Ta

How to tame your PhD

Inger Mewburn, PhD
Thesis Whisperer Books

This book is for Luke, who made it all possible.

This paper edition published Jan, 2012

By Thesis Whisperer Books

Melbourne, 3001

Australia

First published, as ebook only, in September, 2011

www.thesiswhisperer.com

Text: Inger Mewburn

Original cover design: Anitra Nottingham

ISBN 978-1-291-27016-7

ISBN 978-1-291-27016-7

90000

9 781291 270167

There's already a blog, so why a book?

PhD students seem to have become the 'problem children' of academia. Instead of celebrating their incredible contributions, most mainstream media articles focus on the financial and emotional stress of study and the (supposed) lack of jobs at the end of the process. I happen to think doing a PhD is worthwhile and can enrich your life in so many ways, but in my work as a professional research educator I encounter many students who have problems with finishing their PhD and coping with some of the stresses of academic life. The Thesis Whisperer blog (www.thesiswhisperer.com) is dedicated to addressing some of these worries and making some practical suggestions to help you finish faster and with less stress.

I finished my own PhD in 2009, but I have been working with research students since 2006. I know the suggestions in this book work as I put them into practice while I was studying. I finished in three years; one year shorter than most students in Australia. I worked two days a week for all but 7 months of this period, helped to raise a young child and did not get divorced. The finished PhD thesis (those in the US would call this a dissertation) won the faculty award for best thesis at the University of Melbourne, so I know I didn't compromise on quality.

I assure you I am not super human. I firmly believe that anyone who can get into a PhD program in the first place can graduate in a reasonable amount of time and turn out quality work. The trick is to thoroughly understand the nature of the task at hand and use a few simple productivity techniques. In addition, it is important to manage some of the emotions that the PhD experience can provoke. In these pages I will share some of my own strategies – all of which have been talked about at length on the blog.

So why a book if it is all on the blog? You can read most of what is in here for free on the internet, but this ebook is a more linear way to access that content. As a blog grows it eats itself. Posts fall off the front page and tend to be forgotten; new readers find it hard to digest all the material the blog has to offer. This compilation contains more than 20 blog posts which contain essential advice for all research students, regardless of discipline.

I have only included posts which I authored myself. I am lucky to have many people write guest posts for my blog, but have promised faithfully not to publish these in a paid format, so you will have to visit the blog to access them. Many of the posts included here have been altered and edited to improve flow and readability. Extra bridging text has been written to make it more book-like, while not losing the freshness and informality of the blog. You can read this book from start to finish, or in 'chunks' by using the table of contents to jump straight to the topics that interest you most. If you do want to read it straight through, I have arranged the posts loosely around the timeline of the PhD: selecting a topic, understanding the thesis as a form, creative thinking, writing techniques, dealing with procrastination and negative emotions, as well as some tips on editing and presenting your final work.

Please note that the terms I use such as 'thesis' instead of 'dissertation' and 'supervisor' instead of 'advisor' because I teach students immersed in the UK / Australian style of PhD study. Practices vary in the US, Europe and elsewhere but I am confident that most, if not all, of what I have to say will be relevant to PhD students everywhere because it addresses the self directed parts of PhD study, such as the writing of the thesis or dissertation. This book is intentionally short, around 25,000 words. You have enough reading to do as it is. At time of writing the Thesis Whisperer blog contains a further 100,000 words of advice, some of it written by other PhD students. The blog is still active so that store of knowledge is increasing week by week. The comments provided by other PhD students and academics provide interesting extensions and counterpoints. I hope this companion volume will encourage you to explore the blog further.

Why do many people have trouble finishing a PhD?

It is often assumed that PhD students only have themselves to blame for poor completion times and high drop out rates. In my view PhD students are unfairly criticized; often called 'poor communicators', 'abstract thinkers', 'slow writers' or 'bad project managers'. A lot of this is rubbish of course, but the attrition numbers don't lie. Up to one third of those who start their PhD will never finish. It is clear that PhD study is difficult and many students experience a raft of problems along the way, from failed experiments to problems with writing and poor supervision. While many of the problems PhD students are actually problems with the system and academia more generally, the Thesis Whisperer blog wouldn't exist if PhD students didn't face some common issues. I believe it is the outstanding talents that so many PhD students possess which get them into trouble.

It's true that the things we are good at can cause the biggest problems we encounter in life. My friend Colleen worked at a fast food chain as a teenager and was always the one who tasked with mopping the floor at the end of a shift. This was the hardest, nastiest clean up job, which everyone else avoided. When she finally complained to her manager about the constant mopping he replied: "Of course you end up mopping the floor. What do you expect? You're really good at it". There's some wisdom in only being good at the things which you enjoy doing in the workplace!

I like to think about the problems caused by our talents as our own personal Dark Side. As Yoda cautioned Luke Skywalker during the Star Wars Trilogy:"Fear is the path to the dark side. Fear leads to anger. Anger leads to hate. Hate leads to suffering." What Yoda was saying is our natural reactions to events, like fear or anger, if not channeled appropriately, can have unintended consequences. Fallout from your talents can smack you upside your head when you aren't looking. We can even fall into large pools of molten lava if we aren't careful. For example, good researchers are very curious people: they want to KNOW stuff. But to write a thesis you have to learn to channel your curiosity in productively narrow ways.

Many students and academics (including myself) find this narrowing process hard. Curiosity, once unleashed, can be relentless. A person who can't finish their literature review might have a curiosity problem, not a project management problem. They can barely finish reading a paper because they want to dive off in all the other exciting references and directions it suggests. Stopping long enough to write it down is a struggle. Likewise a person who never finishes chapters on time might have an intelligence problem, not a writing problem. PhD students get used to using their intelligence to analyse arguments and look for flaws. The dark side of intelligence creeps in when you start to turn this analytical power onto your own arguments and ideas and find them wanting. A person with an intelligence problem may never think their work is good enough to hand in to the examiner.

Of course part of the process of becoming a scholar is learning how to analyse the strengths and weaknesses of your work. But there's a difference between trying to do good quality work and cutting your own head off with your scholarly light sabre. One of the things I like to do with my students us to give them a series of standard critical thinking questions adapted from Browne and Keeleys' "Asking the Right Questions: A Guide to Critical Thinking":

What is the argument about and what is being claimed?
What are the reasons given to support the conclusion?
Is the reasoning flawed in anyway?
What kind of evidence is being presented (i.e. intuition, appeals to authority, observation, case studies, research studies, analogies, etc) and how good is it?
What other explanations might be plausible than that offered?
Is the conclusion provided the most reasonable? Can you identify alternatives?

Give it a try. You will quickly realise that these critical thinking tools, when they are ruthlessly employed, destroy anything in their path.

So how do we conquer the dark side? I'm with

Yoda on this one - remember that your reactions to the stresses of scholarly life, while natural, are not inevitable and should be examined closely. Understanding that your writing can never be flawless can be strangely liberating. Disagreement and debate is the live blood of academia. There is no way you can be immune to criticism; all you can do is accept it and move on. While we should hold ourselves to high standards, none of us can be perfect all the time. There is no such thing as 'the best' thesis - only good and bad ones.

The role of emotions in PhD Study

Some time ago there was an interesting Thought catalogue blog post entitled "Five emotions invented by the Internet" which made me laugh so hard I snorted the coffee right out of my nose and onto my computer screen. This one was my favourite:

The state of being 'installed' at a computer or laptop for an extended period of time without purpose, characterized by a blurry, formless anxiety undercut with something hard like desperation

Who hasn't felt this way when working to deadline but unable to overcome the urge to check email / twitterfeed / facebook / google scholar or whatever? Since there's something wonderful about discovering others share your own nameless fears and anxieties I started to wonder: what new emotions does a PhD make possible? I decided to test this idea by talking to my PhD student twitter followers. I started by making up my own PhD emotions and sending them out as tweets like so:

Irrational feelings of love for academics you have never met because their work helps you in unexpected ways #phdemotions

For those of you not into twitter, the hashtag (#) enables users to make a 'conversation'. Anyone who included the #tag allows their tweets to be read as part of the same 'thread'. As I hoped, other people followed my lead and started to post their own #phdemotions and a minor meme developed. Later I nerded out and did a content analysis of sorts to see if I could develop a PhD 'mood-o-meter' from all this twitter action (aren't you lucky my employer pays me to do this sort of stuff?).

There ended up being 130 tweets containing either #phdemotion or #phdemotions from the Friday I started the experiment to the following Tuesday. After massaging similar ones together I counted a total of 71 distinct emotional states. If a person really liked the #phdemotion someone else came up with they could retweet it (add it to their 'stream' for others to read) or @mention it (have a conversation with someone else about it). I counted these as a multiplier, which enabled me to make a league table of new emotions.

Using these scientific (ahem) measures for popularity, here are the top 5 emotions made possible by doing a PhD (at least, as determined by PhD students who happened to be on Twitter between the 14th and 18th of January 2011):

Elation when you realise you know more than your supervisor about your topic and you feel brave enough to argue about it: This was an amalgam of tweets by @scientistmags, @soilduck @choloe_kitten. It's not that surprising that this is the most recognised emotion since 'scholarly independence' is meant to be the goal of PhD study. I was happy that a slightly more positive emotion came out on top

Fear of being 'found out' as fraud, not really knowing enough/being smart enough to be Phd student (by @boredpostdoc). Otherwise known as 'the impostor syndrome' and related to the 'Dunning-Kruger effect', this emotion is the result of a demonstrable psychological phenomenon. Put simply, as the old cliché goes: "The more you know, the more you know what you don't know". As well as possibly being related to self-esteem and perfectionism, this emotion could be the by product of the nature and intensity of PhD study itself. PhD students, knowing as much as they do about a subject, are more likely to be aware of the possibility they don't know everything than anyone else.

Unexpected admiration of your own writing. This feeling happens to me sometimes while editing my own work. Apparently it resonates with others too. As @orientalhotel remarked: "That was me yesterday reading my own chapter and thinking, 'yeah good point self'". Usually it applies to text you wrote a year or so ago when you didn't know as much (see above).

The "I'm a genius! Why hasn't anybody thought to do that before?" moment before people point out the

obscure paper you've not read. This emotion surely captures the essence of the PhD emotion roller coaster. Closely related to the emotions described by @wolowic who commented: "experiencing the manic tidal waves of success and complete failure. good & bad stuff happens unbelievably close together!"

Misplaced smugness after photocopying/downloading loads of stuff but not actually reading it (by @orientalhotel). Or as I call it 'Obsessive Article Collecting' syndrome (OACS). This one got a fair bit of discussion, mostly of the 'me too!' variety.

If you have experienced any of these emotions rest assured that you are not alone. Of the list above the only really toxic one is the impostor syndrome. Healthy self-doubt keeps us sharp, but don't let it steal your confidence.

Limiting Self Beliefs

Problems with the system extend beyond the academy and into those ideas about the PhD we pick up from popular culture. Have you ever had that moment at a social function where a relative or friend says: "Wow - you're so smart. I could never do a PhD!" I don't know about you, but the internal dialogue that would inevitably start up in my head would go something like this:

Yes. I AM smart. It's about bloody time Uncle Tim noticed that... But hang on a second Inger. Are you as smart as John? He gave a great presentation the other day didn't he? He's only been doing his PhD for half a year. I have to graduate next year and I clearly haven't read as much as him - or understood it as well. Shit! Calm down woman. You know you can write really, really well. Everything will be ooh-kay. Breathe.... But maybe writing well is not enough? Maybe the examiners will see through my act?

Oh God! I need another slice of cheese cake.

If we are to believe the management and self-empowerment literature, how we think about the world determines our actions in it. Limiting self-beliefs can stop you from achieving your goals (in my case it explains why I gained 17kgs while studying!). Obviously I finished my PhD despite these limiting self-beliefs and most people do; you can talk yourself out of them if you try. The more damaging Limiting Beliefs are the ones that lie 'out there' - by which I mean in academic circles and in popular culture. Here are five beliefs about the PhD that I encounter time and time again in my work. Because they don't come from inside you, it's easier to trapped into believing they are true. Are any of these lurking in your head?

Only the smartest people can do a PhD

One of my favourite TV shows is the Big Bang Theory featuring three PhD and one Masters graduate as main characters. Most of the humour comes from the premise that, although the boys are super smart and endearingly quirky, they don't have much common sense. Shows like this reinforce the myth that people with PhDs are so intelligent that they are somehow alien from the rest of us mortals. Sadly we only have to look around our own faculties and departments to know this isn't true. Success in academia depends on more than 'smarts'. Sometimes it is as basic as being in the right place at the right time or managing your professional networks well. I have seen highly intelligent people fall by the wayside because they got sick of the slog and were smart enough to realise they could make gazillions outside of academia.

I've always been a great student. PhD? No problem!

Success in undergraduate study does not guarantee success in research degree study. A lot of people refuse to believe me when I make this grand statement in workshops, but it's true (refer to any paper or book by US scholar Barbara Lovitts if you don't believe me). Most scholars have come to the conclusion that a complex mix of social and psychological factors account for persistence and resilience in PhD study. Success in undergraduate study usually comes from following rules and passing exams, which don't teach you to be creative or innovative - or develop your emotional maturity. The upside is that you have probably acquired these skills elsewhere: in your professional working life, from hobbies, from parenting and so on. People who come to a PhD later in life often benefit hugely from this 'other' knowledge.

My supervisor is the foremost expert in his field. I can't lose.

How do I say this and not get sued? A great researcher is not always a great supervisor. If someone is at the top of their field they are probably going to be too busy to spend heaps of time reading your work - or soothing your fears. I've even heard of supervisors who have deliberately delayed their students' studies in order to get more results out of them. The good thing about being in academia is that there are many ways to access the knowledge of these 'stars' without having to be in close orbit. You can read their papers, meet them at conferences or email them questions. If you are lucky they might peer review one of your journal papers. Stars are great examiners because if they like your work they are in a position to help you with your career. So don't worry if your supervisor is not a star. Do worry if they are inexperienced - but I'll get to that later on.

Writing a dissertation is just like writing a book - yes?

No. Popular non-fiction draws the reader into another world; it doesn't spend time convincing the reader how smart the author is. A thesis is a peculiar kind of document; one which is meant to demonstrate your scholarly competence, not to entertain. Pick up any popular science or history book and you will see the difference immediately. Gone are the brackets containing references. Gone are phrases like "The literature suggests..." Even academic books are an unhelpful frame of reference; it's rare for an academic book to contain a whole chapter dedicated to methodology for example. Besides, thinking you have to produce the definitive tome on some subject or other is daunting. Better writing models for your thesis can be found by reading journal papers in your area. By all means write a book - but later, when you can put (PhD) after your name on the cover.

I've never heard of anyone failing their PhD, therefore it can't happen.

I'm not sure about the US, but you can fail your PhD in Australia and the UK. It only happens to a vanishingly small percentage of people so it's unlikely to happen to you (especially if you are the kind of student who bothers to read this book!). At our institution the majority of students have to make changes before they can pass and up to 5% of people have to do major revisions, or even be re-examined. This can mean up to a year of extra study with all the hassle and pain that suggests. Be vigilant about these self-limiting beliefs and never assume that 'what everyone knows' is necessarily true, or true for you.

Finding the right topic

It surprises many people who haven't done a PhD that it can be hard to know what your topic really is. When you first start a PhD your ideas can shift around a lot; it may seem like from week to week you change your mind. Over time you would hope this situation would settle down, but I meet many people who have two or more topics struggling to be in the same thesis, right up to the last minute.I call this the Incredible Hulk Complex: too much man, too little shirt (your poor thesis text is the shirt in this metaphor by the way).

I am no stranger to the Incredible Hulk complex. I originally got into a PhD program proposing that I would investigate the use of genetic algorithms in architectural design. I ended up looking at how architects use gesture as they are designing together.

It was hard to let go of all the interests that I had but, to paraphrase what a J.R.R Tolkien once wrote, there can be only One ~~Ring~~ Topic. Only one Topic can rule them all, find them, bring them all and in the darkness bind them. My supervisor gets the credit for convincing me to do work on gesture - and he has my undying thanks. How do you know when you have the One Topic? Here's how I knew:

I found there was substantial work in the area already

This may run counter to the idea that a thesis has to be an 'original contribution to knowledge', but there's doable-original and too-original. If some work in the area exists already you have something to hold onto, examine and critique if necessary. When I decided to look at gesture I naively thought there wouldn't be much work on it - how wrong was I! There was about 200 years of research in the area of gesture already. I found this demoralising until I realised that only about 3 people had looked at architects and none had looked at education in the same way I was - a nice little gap was still left for me to squeeze into.

I thought it was fascinating

Gesture is a compulsive thing - you can't help doing it. When you think about it as you do it, it becomes really hard to talk. Give it a try and you'll see what I mean. Did you know that even blind people gesture? They gesture when they are on the phone - to other blind people! If we gesture to communicate with others, why would blind people do it? Obviously I still find gesture mysterious and fascinating, even after three years of looking at it. This curiosity and desire to know kept me going. When all else looked bleak and I was slamming doors in my house in a fit of PhD rage I could always return to and draw from this well of curiosity. I really don't think I could have finished without this thirst to know. I know that sounds dorky, but that's how it was.

Other people said "wow - what a great topic" when I told them

Apart from one of the mothers at my son's school who said with genuine disbelief "What the hell would you want to study that for!?" everyone else I talked to about my topic found it interesting. Especially (and this is the most important thing) all the architecture academics in my faculty, my home university and at conferences I went to. Since academics found it interesting they would remember that I was doing it and send me articles. Lots of people would come to my seminars when I had work to present. I got a lot of help from others, I think because they genuinely wanted to know what I would find out.

It wasn't too hot

Genetic algorithms in architecture used to be HOT. Who remembers that now? God - so early 2000's... Gesture however is timeless. Others may dispute my findings, build on my work, dismiss it, but it will always be part of the discourse. It's impossible for every topic to be timeless. Scientists' work is unlikely to be relevant for more than 3 years. If it can't be timeless it is good to work in a field that has the potential develop further, so you can still be a part of it as it moves on.

It had clear limits

This point relates back to point one. Since there was work in the field already there were pre-existing boundaries to the work I could do and stay 'original'. Since I decided to focus on a location (gesture in architectural education) there was a lot that didn't have to make it in to the thesis. The topic acted like a sieve, which only certain things passed through.

What is a thesis or dissertation?

We can learn a lot about the problems of writing a PhD thesis or dissertation from studying the medieval origins of doctoral study. One book I particularly like is William Clark's "Academic charisma and the origins of the research University". It's an excellent book, but odd and self-consciously post-modern and therefore hard to read. Most PhD students would never bother, which is a pity because it lays out a fascinating argument about doctoral scholars and how they became progressively 'disembodied' into text. Clark's book provides a useful way to think about becoming a doctor because it explains (I think) some of the oddities of the thesis/dissertation process and emphasises the importance of authorship.

In a nutshell, Clark's argument is that back in the day (around 500 years ago) if you wanted to be a Doctor (in a Western Europe context) all you had to do was know everything. Luckily this was relatively easy because back then people believed that everything there was to know was written in the Bible. The Bible was the official canon of knowledge; in order to graduate to doctor-hood you studied it closely for a long period of time and then took part in a public process called the 'disputation'.

Basically the disputation was an academic performance piece that acted as a rite of passage – the only one we have left today is the graduation ceremony. Clark calls the Disputation a 'knowledge 'joust': the student stood up in public and defended the canon of knowledge in the Bible against a series of 'unorthodox' suggestions. The suggestions usually came from a crowd of your peers (who had been appropriately clued up about the kind of unorthodox suggestions you had answers for - probably over a pint of mead or two in the local pub). Your teacher stood behind you while you fielded the 'heterodoxy' from the crowd and refuted it with Syllogistic logic. Seated around the sides of the rooms were professors and and even local nobles who were the official witnesses to the event. These people decided if your performance in this academic punching match meant you were worthy to become doctor.

So becoming doctor used to be a thoroughly fleshy affair in which you demonstrated your scholarly capabilities in public and in person. But with the invention of the printing press everything began to change. Clark takes some 300 pages to explain how the disputation system, which relied on speaking received knowledge in public, changed to the circulation of papers. This circulation took place in private because the text started to be written for a select group of scholars (the disciplines) instead of for all scholars.The text started to embody the scholar; it became the authorised way to speak knowledge. I like to think about the text in terms of the movie Avatar - a movie I happened to like despite all the criticisms (mostly because of Sigourney Weaver -what's not to love?!). A thesis text is like an avatar. It 'stands in' for your scholarly self and 'speaks' your knowledge and capability as a scholar to the reader / examiner when you aren't there. The examiner, as the most important reader, is like the witnesses to the old disputation; they decide if your text avatar is good enough at speaking knowledge to be considered a doctor.

Your scholarly capabilities must be translated into the medium of text. This is not an easy feat. As Sam Worthington discovered, things are different when you become an avatar. You have different capabilities because you take a different form; you both gain and lose in this transformation. Before you think I have gone off into post modernist la-la-land, this transformation has some practical implications. For one thing texts say lots of things but they are really mute. Think about the examiner in the act of reading your text - they may come across something they think is wrong or something they disagree with. They may well wonder aloud why you haven't done something, or said something. They may want to ask you if you understand some nuance or other. But unless you have thought of this possibility beforehand - and put it in the text - there will be no answer. You are only a ghostly presence in your text avatar. It has to speak *for* you.

This is why it's important that the thesis text is very, very good. Or as I like to think about it: big, blue, strong and sexy.

The dead hand of the thesis genre

There are many conventions about how a thesis should be structured and formatted. These vary slightly, but not as much as you may expect, over disciplines. There are plenty of books to give you advice on these standard formats so I am not going to labour too much here (a good primer is "How to write a better thesis" by Evans, Gruba and Zobel).[1] While the conventions are laid out in detail in these books, there is little to no discussion of their effects on the writer – you. As with any convention, what starts off as a good idea becomes stifling when it is applied too zealously. Many students do not lack the skills or knowledge to write a document in the conventional way but many find they suffer under what we like to call in my workplace the 'dead hand of the thesis genre'.

There are two dead hands actually: conventional thesis structure, known as the 'IMRAD' formula (introduction - methods - results - discussion), and a certain kind of 'scholarly style of language': mannered, distancing, defensive and lacking the personal pronoun ('I'). Maybe it is unfair for us to call it the dead hand of the thesis genre, because there are certainly a few disciplines where the IMRAD structure and scholarly language of the distancing variety are a pair of warm and lively hands which help you to get the job done. This is because there is a deep and abiding connection between this conventional way of doing a thesis and the scientific method. The IMRAD formula follows the experimental method cycles and the language is designed to present the results as facts, which exist apart from the researcher.

In the scientific method the questions are raised before the experiments designed to answer them. Sure fresh questions will probably emerge as the scientific work progresses, but always to drive a new cycle of research. In other disciplines, this is not the case. Research questions may not be known in advance or may change substantially during the research - they may only emerge clearly at the very end. There will not necessarily be experiments to generate data, but observations, interviews, painting, the making of car engines and so on. There are many different ways of making knowledge where ideas, data and arguments are unlikely to fit easily into the conventional thesis formula - yet some students feel compelled to torture them until they do. You may not set out to replicate this type of conventional thesis and still find that the dead hand is resting upon you because you freeze up when you try to write something 'real' - not jottings in a notebook.

At my university we get three other kinds of thesis that do not follow the IMRAD formula: the 'big book thesis' (common to history and social sciences), the 'bunch of papers' (a collection of published articles, becoming popular in the sciences) and the creative exegesis (text accompanying art and design projects). When there is this variety, why has the IMRAD formula, so necessary in the sciences, come to haunt the rest of us?

There's a good discussion of this issue in an article called "Thesis and dissertation writing: an examination of published advice and actual practice" by Brian Paltridge who examined some 30 finished PhDs to see how closely they aligned with the type of advice given in the 'how to do a PhD' books. The findings were preliminary as the sample set was small, but I think the observations were interesting nonetheless. Paltridge starts by analysing a range of texts available on the subject of thesis and dissertation writing. He includes some classics, such as Phillips & Pugh's "How to get a PhD", through to the eternally useful "How to write a thesis" by Evans and Gruba as well as some less well known ones. Paltridge found these books vary as to the amount of advice that they give on the overall organisation of a thesis, but all are light on when it comes to suggestions about structure. Some of the less useful ones devote as little as 3 pages to the issue.

   Paltridge claims that most authors, when they do discuss structure, tend to outline the 'IMRAD' formula in simple or more complex forms. Virtually none of the 'how to' books provided advice on other ways of structuring a thesis, most likely because the author is trying to address multiple disciplines. The 'how to' genre needs to be read with this issue front of mind; more specific advice will often needed. Hopefully your supervisor will be in a position to provide this. While there are some books that talk explicitly about structure (one of my favourites is "Authoring a PhD" by Patrick Dunleavy who writes advice specifically for the 'big book' thesis writers) they are few and far between, perhaps because publishers worry they wont sell enough. The fall back advice is to look to examples of passed theses for models for your thesis. While this can be useful, I would add the caveat that the authors of these finished theses or dissertations would revise them given half the chance - I know I would.

So if you find yourself being pressed under the dead hand of the thesis genre remember that the summary judgment of your thesis by the examiner will be made on how well your thesis 'sings the song' of the content within it. Your job is to make that song lively, not a funeral dirge.

How to Fail your PhD

In Australia most theses are examined through blind peer review. Other countries have different ways of doing examination, but in every system judgment of any PhD is the job of a small group of experts. This is an assessment process unlike any other in academe and it pays to be familiar with it. You'll be pleased to know that people have spent time studying how examiners read a thesis and what sort of document they expect you to deliver. The seminal paper is "It's a PhD, not a Nobel Prize: how experienced examiners assess research theses" by Gerry Mullins and Margaret Kiley. I consider this paper required reading for every research student, regardless of their location or discipline. There's a lot I could say about this paper. In fact I have been talking about this paper for about 5 years in one of my On Track Workshops "What do examiners really want?" where I spend two hours examining it in detail.

As you can imagine this is one of our more popular sessions, but I must admit I'm beginning to feel like one of those aged rock stars. Although the audience expects it, I don't want to sing a straight version of my hit wonder from the 1980s. I want to sing songs from my new album. So here I turn around my normal presentation of the paper. If Mullins and Kiley are right about how examiners examine - what are 5 things you could do if you really wanted to fail (or at least be asked to do major revisions)?

Don't talk to your supervisor about the examination

I am located in the School of Graduate Research. We are the unit at RMIT University who manage the examination process, so I get to read a lot of examiner reports and see the occasional complaint go by. By far and away the most common complaint is that the examiner didn't understand what the student was trying to do. Usually this means there's some kind of disagreement about method and how the student has handled (or not) validity, reliability and so on. You don't have to know exactly who the examiners are, but you do need to know if the supervisor is thinking about the right kinds of people. There aren't too many academics that are truly broadminded. It's best if you have someone who will be sympathetic to your methodology. Sometimes supervisors take the confidential nature of the examination process seriously and may brush off your attempts to have a conversation about what sort of people they have in mind. However most universities allow you to nominate a list of people who would **not** be appropriate. In my opinion every student should send a list of inappropriate people to their supervisor - if only for the record.

Just in case ok? Humour me

Send your thesis to someone who has never examined a thesis before

Mullins and Kiley found that even more than methodological orientation, the amount of experience the examiner has matters in the way they come to a judgment. This probably makes sense to those of you who teach. Young teachers tend to have high expectations because they haven't had time to see the full range of student ability. The longer you teach, the more forgiving you become because for every new student you encounter, you have probably seen another who was worse. Some people can be nervous about sending their thesis to the world's expert in *blah*, but they are exactly the sort of people you should be aiming for.

Write your introduction first

One of the most interesting and useful observations Mullins and Kiley made is that most examiners don't read your thesis like it's a novel - starting at the beginning and reading through to the end. Shocked? I was the first time I read this, but then I reflected on the last academic book I read from start to finish... and I couldn't think of one. Academic texts are dense, difficult, cumbersome beings at the best of times and a thesis is even worse. Most examiners read the abstract, introduction and the conclusion to see what the work is about and then look in the references, so you should write these last - or rather rewrite them at the end.

Any questions you raise in the introduction should be answered in the conclusion. If these parts act as righteous 'bookends' the examiner will form a better impression of you as a scholar - and is likely to be more forgiving of you if you slip up a bit in the middle parts.

Write a bad literature review

Oh boy. Where do I start? There are so many ways to write a bad literature review that it deserves a few posts on its own. The literature review is the nice party frock of your thesis. If the examiner sees that you have chosen the right frock for the occasion they are more likely to want to have a drink with you. It goes without saying your frock should be freshly ironed and have no stains on it - even better if it matches your handbag and shoes.

The kind of dress you think is appropriate is up to you, but I think you can't go wrong with a little black dress (LBD). In thesis land the LBD is a simple, but competent run through of the major authors with a thread of an argument running through the whole. The argument should be connected to why you are bothering to do the study.

It's up to you of course, you can be more daring, but I would stop short of trying to be Lady Gaga.

Don't let anyone else do your copy-editing

Mullins and Kiley note that across all disciplines examiners report being put off by 'sloppiness'. Yep - typos, missed footnotes, badly formatted bibliographies and so on. Those of you writing in a different language don't need to fret too much, there's evidence to suggest that examiners accommodate idiosyncratic grammar more than plain mess. I'm not sure how much it costs to get a copy editor - but most universities will allow you to employ one under certain guidelines. If not, do a lot of favours for a grammar enabled friend and ask them to perform the duty for you. It's hard to see the mistakes in your own work on the 700th read.

Why you might be Stuck

In high school I had a history teacher who would talk about the second world war like he was a German soldier. At first his performance was funny. In his hands every victory by the allies became a loss; every weakness of the allies was celebrated and German losses were lamented. But as the year went on and we learned about the extermination of the Jews, I became increasingly outraged and confused. My teacher seemed to regard these atrocities lightly and have perverse admiration for the German war machine. Was he some kind of escaped Nazi war criminal, or merely deluded? I began to dread history classes, but I didn't say anything because – well – it was not my place to question the teacher.

One day however I couldn't take it any more and finally put my hand up. I asked him why he thought the Germans were so great. Surely the Allies weren't all that hopeless. They had won the war hadn't they? By way of an answer he started telling us his story of fleeing from Europe with his parents at the start of the war. *Then he told us he was a Jew.*

I realised I was being treated to a fiendishly clever teaching strategy. He was showing us that all history is a story told by someone for a particular purpose. He finished his lecture by asking us: "After this

how do you know anything said by a teacher is true?"
This question hit me right in the stomach. I was 16, but
(sadly) this is the first time I realised a teacher could
consciously choose – or even be forced - to *lie*.
Simultaneously I realised how conditioned I was to
believing teachers unquestioningly. I can honestly say
this moment changed my life. I felt liberated. I didn't
have to believe my teachers anymore! But, for the rest of
high school I found learning exhausting and sometimes
deeply unsettling. Reluctantly (I was 16 after all and
wanted to be thinking about boys at that point) I started
to question everything anyone told me – including my
parents. Did they *know* what they were saying was true,
or only *believe* it? Were they trying to trick me?

Prof Jan Meyer, professor of education, would
say that when I realised that teachers could lie I
encountered, and crossed over, a 'threshold concept': this
insight once grasped was unforgettable. It made me see
the world in a new and transformed way. As is common
with this kind of learning, before I crossed the threshold
concept I had been 'stuck', unable even to give voice to
my questions. After I crossed the threshold the insight I
gained was integrative. It caused other knowledge I had
been exposed to fall into place; knowledge about history,
the school system, my place in it and even the nature of
truth and belief, good and evil. But this changed
knowledge led to a changed self and was therefore
troublesome. Learning was no longer routine, but
question filled and uncertain.

Being 'stuck' is a common experience in doing a

PhD, which often manifests as a difficulty in writing. Sometimes it is hard to know why you are stuck, or how to get over it. It could be that you are facing a threshold concept without realising it. Researchers Margaret Kiley and Gina Wisker have studied this problem and came to the remarkable conclusion that certain PhD threshold concepts are consistent across all disciplines. These manifest as a common set of struggles:

Struggle to understand that a thesis is a claim or defence – not just a collection of work you have done or a way of proving existing beliefs.

Struggle to be able to articulate a position on 'the literature' or locate the work you are doing within it

Struggle to develop a theory or a model which allows the findings to be used, or applied to other cases.

But I think threshold concepts can be more modest, mundane affairs. You may become stuck because you need to unlearn certain ways of doing things. For instance, a research student wrote to me thanking me for a sudden insight. He used to be a computer programmer. He realised that he had become 'stuck' because he had unconsciously approached research writing in the same way. He had been trying to plan out all his chapters before writing them as he would a program. As a result he was becoming disheartened at the size and difficulty of the task. My description of myself as a messy writer suddenly provoked a simple, but powerful, realization: he could write 'chunks' of his thesis, without necessarily knowing what was coming next.

In grasping this he has realised something important about the whole process of research. Sometimes you don't have to know what the outcome of a process will be – you just have to do it and see what happens. It is hard for a supervisor to help a student through such a block because they are not always visible in the student's behaviour. As the psychologist RD Laing it:

> He does not think there is anything the matter
> with him because
> one of the things that *is* the matter with him
> is that he does not *think* there is anything the
> matter with him

A lot of the advice on doing a PhD does not recognise these conceptual blocks. Many treat doing a thesis like a project which has to be 'managed', not a difficult and troublesome learning process. Research degree learning involves encountering and changing some deeply habitual ways of operating and thinking. The project management approach doesn't always work. Unfortunately, when it doesn't, it's all too easy to blame yourself for not working 'efficiently' – when this isn't the problem you need to solve. Even if you recognise the problem, crossing a threshold means you will probably encounter 'troublesome' knowledge. For our computer programmer the realisation that a thesis must be written 'messily' will not be easy to live with. Writing messily means you produce a lot of excess that has to be pared back.

I think the idea of 'threshold concepts' helps us think more positively about 'being stuck'. Being stuck can be a sign you are becoming aware that you are, as Jack Mezirow put it, 'caught in your own history'. A good way to move forward is to ask yourself: "Is there anything I need to unlearn?"

How to cook up ideas

A PhD thesis or dissertation is supposed to make a "significant and original contribution to knowledge". This can create a lot of angst amongst research students, partly because originality is often defined, but rarely talked about in actionable ways.

In "How to get a PhD", Phillips and Pugh set out 16 ways to be original (page 62 of the current edition if you are interested), but don't say anything at all about how to come up with the original ideas in the first place. Similarly "Doctorates Downunder", edited by Evans and Denholm, has chapters full of useful suggestions for managing your time and enriching your study experience that may increase your chances of finishing your doctorate, they do not really help you become original. Don't get me wrong - it is good to know what originality *means* in relation to doing a PhD, but it's far better to know what you have to *do* to produce enough original and novel ideas to fill a thesis.

The reason why so many books avoid this topic, perhaps rightly so, is that creativity is assumed to be a disciplinary issue or an individual matter. Either you know enough about your subject to see the way to produce novel ideas, or you are naturally a creative person who will come up with them anyway. But is this really the case? Are there actions you can take that can help you come up with more ideas and solutions to research problems - regardless of discipline?

You may have figured out by now that I have a fascination with the issue of creativity in research - how it happens, how to promote it and how to think about it. This is why I enjoyed reading a paper that attempts to measure social interconnectedness and the relationship with ideas generation called "Social origins of good ideas" by Ronald Burt explored the production and uptake of good ideas in a supply chain logistics company by exploring the nature of discussion networks amongst managers. He found that the network in the company was characterised by a 'bridge and cluster' formation. Most people discussed ideas with their immediate work colleagues (within clusters) but relatively few people would act as 'bridgers' and talk to colleagues across clusters. Managers who had a diverse social network, ie: those who 'bridged' between clusters of smaller discussion networks were "at risk of having more good ideas".

Bert supports this argument by a whole bunch of numbers that seem pretty convincing to me. Although I could probably drive a truck through this method on the grounds that he doesn't really into account physical objects and locations and how they affect social relationships, or give much attention to how generalisable this knowledge is, given that a logistics company is bound to have some unique constraints, I think the findings are interesting nonetheless.

The hypothesis that lies behind this work is that, within a discussion cluster, information, beliefs and behaviours tend to become more homogenous over time. This is certainly a phenomenon one sees if they work for any period of time in the same office or live in a family group. Burt's key argument is that 'bridgers' discuss ideas with a wide range of people, not just the ones closest to hand. As a consequence they are more likely to be exposed to contradictory ideas and alternative practices. If these bridgers are astute and thoughtful, they can see ways to transfer or combine ideas and approaches from elsewhere to their own problems.

In effect, Burt claims, "Creativity is an import export business". A mundane idea in one area can be a spectacular one in another because the recipient determines the value of the idea, not the person who thinks it up. Burt argues that: "the certain path to being creative is to find a constituency more ignorant than yourself" and notes that this is a common tactic in academia (!)

Here's where it gets interesting for you. Think about it for a moment: what do you spend most of your time on while doing your PhD? Probably doing experiments, making stuff (or whatever it is you do) and/or reading the work of others. Hopefully you will also be hanging out with your peers and talking to your supervisors.

These are good ways of generating ideas, but could you be doing more? Administrators and academics in my university constantly complain that it's hard to convince PhD students to attend lunchtime seminars put on by other researchers. When I was doing my PhD it always seemed like a waste of time to break my flow and attend such events unless I knew the person who was presenting, or the topic of the seminar seemed especially relevant. I always assumed that the discussion was unlikely to have any direct relevance - but what about indirect relevance? Might I have missed out on many opportunities to cross breed exciting new idea hybrids?

So I will finish with some questions for us to ponder. How can you create an ideas 'import export' business? How much time do you spend in discussion about ideas with others? Who are they? Do you need to find more people who will expose you to different ways of thinking and doing? Since no one likes a free loader, what might people in these other areas learn from you?

Taming the Literature Dragon

The literature review is the thesis component that
gives you the most scope to demonstrate your mad skills
of scholarly warfare. Being able to write a killer
literature review is important because it 'sells' your
academic competence to examiners and other readers.
The literature review receives a lot of attention in
the how-to-do-a-PhD books. The key point they all make
is that the lit review must be more than a list of things
you read – it has to have an argument and a point of
view. There's no shortage of good advice out there, such
as this excellent list of 'literature moves' out of my
favourite book on PhD writing, "Helping doctoral
students to write":

Sketch out the nature of the field relevant to the inquiry –
including history if relevant and

Identify major debates and define terms, in order to,

Establish which studies, ideas and/or methods are most
pertinent to your study, and

Locate gaps in the field, in order to

Create a warrant for the study in question, and

Identify the contribution the study might make

But there's a gap between this kind of style advice and the actual mechanics of analysing and organising the raw material of your literature review. I'm talking about getting to grips with all those journal articles people. You have rather a lot of them don't you? How are you going to 'identity major debates' and decide which are the 'right' studies to draw on in all that mess?

As I see it, there are two basic techniques for developing a literature review from a given set of references. You must work at forming critical judgment on the literature by reading it, at the same time as you work on finding patterns in the mess of information. It's important to realise that these patterns are not 'real' – you make them by sorting and presenting the information in particular ways. This sorting process makes the raw information *legible* so that you can start to write an argument from it. This is more than a filing problem.

If you are anything like me you have a massive pile of journal articles on your desk. The neat freaks amongst you will have them all printed out and filed in alphabetized binders. Some of the more technical minded amongst you will probably be using something like Mendeley or even – ahem – Endnote. These tools help you find stuff when you want it, but they don't do the intellectual heavy lifting for you.

There are many different techniques you can use

to massage meaning out of your information mess, but there's only room here for one. It comes from the seminal book 'Information Anxiety' by Richard Saul Wurzman. Yes, you heard right – Wurzman is the creator of the TED talks (good pedigree I think!). Wurzman argues that there are only 5 ways to organise information, which he calls LATCH: **L**ocation, **A**lphabet, **T**ime, **C**ategory and **H**ierarchy. These organising principles can be used to perform simple operations on the material you have. Here are some ideas.

Location

All scholars are 'located' somehow. Sometimes geography matters – think of the famous 'Chicago school' in social science. But we can think about location in more abstract ways – such as a 'location' of a scholar within a discipline. Some scholars will be 'fringe' and others will be 'main actors'; some people will be 'theoretical' and others will be 'practical'; some people will care about history, others will not – and so on. Make a table in word and arrange the authors according to different 'locations'. This is a good way of choosing which authors you can use to illustrate the dimensions of each debate. It's easy to compare and contrast their ideas with each other because you have identified oppositions.

Alphabet

Of course alphabet is essential to organising your bibliography! I can't think of another good use for alphabetical in a literature review, so I'll pass over this one for my favourite:

Time

Simple genius. Take all the references and lay them out on the floor in order of their publishing date from left to right (or whichever way your culture prefers to do it). Skim read them all again in order – what do you notice? Fashions will have come and gone; ideas will have grown and died. This is a really good way of interrogating underlying assumptions in a body of literature and how they have developed. Indeed you may discover that 'facts' presented by subsequent authors are merely 'ideas' which have grown pretensions by being repeated by subsequent authors, who haven't done due diligence like you have.

Category

I call this the 'colour by numbers' technique and use it often as a quick and dirty method of squeezing sense out of the literature. Basically you can develop categories about almost any idea or theme you read about. A good way to come up with themes is to visualise them in a spider diagram. Once you have identified the categories they can act as subheadings in your literature chapter. Simply make a list of which authors fit in which categories; don't worry if some of them occupy multiple categories – that can be solved with:

Hierarchy

I find this organisational principle is really a 'meta' device – a way of criticising information you have already sorted using one of the other methods, particularly the category method. You make a hierarchy by exerting critical judgment on each of your categories: is one school of thought or way of doing things described in the literature superior to the others? Is one idea more practical and useful than another idea – or more theoretically interesting and elegant? Why? If you have organised your information according to location and identified oppositions, you can use hierarchies to identify which side you are on in the various debates. As you write, you weave in the critical stance you have developed – but that's a topic for another time.

So that's a grab bag of techniques to tame your literature dragon – at the very least they give you something to do when you are stuck!

The problem of 'productivity'

I think and write a lot about time and work; specifically how there never seems to be enough of the former to do all of the latter. My life is full of family, work and side hobby projects as it is, when I have large projects on at work I find myself getting increasingly anxious. At 4am my mind races: how am I going to get this thing done? For years I felt it as a constant, background hum to my life. I call this feeling Thesis Panic. Thesis panic is caused by what seems like an impossibly large and difficult project coupled with a fast approaching deadline. Reactions to Thesis Panic vary. Some people are good at calm acceptance, while others, like me, walk around with stomach churning anxiety that makes us distracted, irritable and hard to live with.

Certainly it does help to adopt structured work habits when you are doing a thesis. When I was studying friends and colleagues with PhDs advised me to treat the whole process like a job. "Keep regular hours" one person said to me at a party - "and write everyday". "Treat your supervisor like a boss" recommended another over a cup of coffee, "think about what makes them look good and do it". I took this advice to heart, put it into practice and found it worked: I finished in three years, while working part time for most of it. But treating the thesis like a job didn't minimise my anxiety very much, if at all. While I was going through these 'job like' motions at no time did doing the thesis really feel like a job - at least not a job as I understood it. For one thing I thought about my thesis all the time, even in my off hours - and the thinking made me either excited to get an idea on paper Right Now, or anxious. Sometimes it was hard to tell the difference between the two feelings, but towards the end the anxiety took over and didn't lift until the day I got my examiner reports back.

It is hard - very hard - to talk yourself out of Thesis Panic, but it can help to talk to other people about it. While you might think the best people to talk to are those who are the calm types, I'm not so sure. They say the worst students make the best teachers because they really know what it is like to struggle. I found it far more comforting to talk to other sufferers - at least I felt less alone with the feeling.

In my work I see lots of cases of Thesis Panic, but mostly in a professional setting. I have been lucky enough to have family and close friends do research degrees, which has given me the opportunity to observe the phenomenon close up and personal. I've murmured a lot of soothing words in phone calls, had many therapeutic cups of tea and proof read many paragraphs which the writer was too anxious to show their supervisor. Along the way I've been able to talk to each of them about what they are feeling and why. This has helped me to understand the phenomenon a bit better.

For instance, I was telling my sister how

implementing my 1000 words strategy instantly calmed me, whereas when I was doing thesis, it didn't have the same soothing effect. She pointed out some fundamental differences between doing general academic work, like writing journal articles, and doing a thesis.

Firstly, while managers or colleagues may offer opinions on my work or give me directions, but they are not making a summary judgment about whether or not I get a PhD. Secondly work boundaries of a book are more likely to be known and agreed on in advance. In my job for example, my manager and I set out in writing an agreement at the start of each year what projects I will be involved in and what the deadlines are. Most thesis writers don't have the luxury of certainty. Experiments may fail, data may be useless, theories may not hold together and so on. It's possible to find yourself staring down the barrel of the deadline with no thesis, multiple possible theses or a very tenuous thesis. The anxiety is not something you can necessarily get rid of because most of the reasons for it are external and, to some extent at least, out of your control.

Treating problem of doing a thesis as just a matter of 'work' explains why productivity techniques only go so far in helping people overcome an attack of Thesis Panic. Time management is a concept invented in the industrial age and designed to help people run factories, not intellectual work. Although I am a big fan of productivity literature and the tools it describes, they don't necessarily hold all the answers to finishing your thesis in a timely fashion. You should take any of what I say next about productivity with a grain of salt. Try these techniques and see if they work for you, but don't beat yourself up if they don't work all the time.

Your writing tools

There are deep and subtle connections between research thinking and research writing. Most people don't notice how much these writing and thinking are shaped by the kinds of tools that are used to carry them out. The Philosopher Michel Foucault claimed (and please forgive the drastic simplification those of you who are steeped in the subtleties of Foucault) the way we think and act is always shaped by the action of other people and things. Paying attention to the tools you use and working out ways to hack them to work better for you pays dividends in terms of time and frustration.

The tools don't have to be actual things; for example, you can use simple techniques to make your writing into a better tool for thinking. In the book "They say / I say: the moves that matter in persuasive writing" Graff and Birkenstein argue that critical thinking and writing can be aided by using writing 'skeletons'; sentences which set up a standard piece of argumentation.

For example, the following sentences could be seen as a 'kit of parts' for thinking through the work of others – just fill in the blanks:

The evidence about *[blank]* shows that *[blank]*

The findings of *[blank]* have important consequences for the broader domain of *[blank]*

"The standard way of thinking about *[blank]* has it that *[blank]*

In making this point I am challenging the common belief that *[blank]*

You can make your own templates by stripping out words from papers you read. Is this plagiarism? No, because we academics rely on conventional forms of writing and speaking to be understood within our respective disciplines; they don't belong to anyone in particular. If you make and use scaffolds they can help you form different writing habits. Like encouraging a vine to grow over a trellis, over time, the ways of thinking your writing scaffolds encourage become habitual. You will find that words start to come out of your hands 'pre-fabricated' in an academically legible way.

One reason that writing is such a good thinking tool is that it encourages us to think in a linear fashion, one word in front of the other. By writing sentences and building paragraphs we express ideas and chain them together into a coherent argument. Once our ideas are in writing we can reflect on them and add the evidence, definitions, side arguments and all the other embellishments that give our arguments weight and heft.

This linear, methodical way of thinking through writing is a good thing - most of the time. However many people find they can only sustain a linear mode of writing for about 1500 words. Certainly this is the case for me. I can write about 2 pages at most before I have to stop and review where I am going. You may be able to go for longer, but inevitably, if you keep working words in a straight line, your arguments will start to lose coherence.

When you are stuck in the line by line, word by word business of writing it is easier to lose sight of overall purpose; how the part we are writing relates to the whole. I have never yet met anyone capable of writing a whole 90,000 thesis in this stream of consciousness / linear way (but feel free to write to me if you have!). To re-orient during the writing process most of us will stop to read back what we have written. The danger here is Editing. Too much editing at the initial drafting stage is, more often than not, the enemy of Done.

Robyn Owens, in the excellent (if badly named) book Doctorates Down-under', calls this editing-as-you-go 'the spiral method' of writing. She warns that the spiral method, while good for creating coherence, can lead to the 'one step forward, two steps back' problem where work is done - but little real progress is made. You probably have experienced this: found yourself opening your document, tinkering around with the first couple of paragraphs for what seems like five minutes, then looking up to see it is already lunchtime.

A whiteboard gives you a different kind of space

to work your ideas - a way to draw back and seek out higher ground from which to survey your whole thesis or chapter. On a whiteboard you are not committed in quite the same way as you are in a word processor. Ideas seem more playful, tentative and open. On a whiteboard you can draw diagrams, which can help you to arrange ideas in novel ways. Of course you can do this on paper, but on a whiteboard it is easier to rub stuff out and move things around. One of my favourite whiteboard tricks is the 'clustering' or 'spider' diagram:

In the diagram above I started with a central bubble called 'Research Student Experience'. The next step is to try literally 'draw out' sub themes or related ideas in new bubbles connected with 'legs' to the original bubble. The next set of 'legs' contains references to papers that talk about each of these aspects of the research experience.

This diagramming method enables me to find relations between the ideas and the authors that I am reading - great for lit reviews. Each of the bubbles might simply translate to a subheading in your thesis or paper. By keeping one idea in the centre and forcing yourself to stick to only three ideas the next bubble layer down you impose a hierarchy on your thoughts. You can work through ideas for structure quickly in this way, perhaps taking a photo of each one before you rub it out so you have a record.

Tools have the most influence on our thinking and writing when we think they are not affecting us. The bird that sits in the cage even when the door is open has failed to notice the cage anymore; the bird accepts its imprisonment not as an action of a cage, or an owner, but as a simple fact of existence. So it is with Microsoft Word I am sorry to say. Put simply, over the years Microsoft Word 'domesticated' me. I started to think and do things the way it wanted me to and I didn't even notice how it cramped my style until I stopped using it in preference for Scrivener - a word processor that works in quite a different way.

There are several different alternatives to Word on the market, but rarely do people think of using any other software to do the heavy lifting, despite MS Word's obvious deficiencies. Here are five reasons why you might consider changing to something like Scrivener:

Humans don't think don't think like typewriters

I haven't studied this, but I'm pretty sure when the first word processors were developed they modelled the action of typewriters – a series of 'blank' pages waiting to have words stamped on them. But a typewriter is not like a human; it doesn't think as it writes. If Microsoft Word conceptualises a document as sequential paper sheets which you 'stamp' words on; Scrivener sees your writing as a loose collection of fragments that can be modified and rearranged as you go. When you are done fiddling around you can 'compile' the fragments to produce a linear document. This is an elegant idea that recognises that it is extremely difficult to write complex document like a thesis 'straight'. It's helpful to start by working smaller pieces in parallel and then work out how they go together.

It's hard to be messy in a clean way

As I write I have ideas; some don't relate to the bit I am writing at that specific moment, so I 'tend to jot notes on my documents as I go. I used to use the comments function in Word, which made my documents look messy. In fact, comments made my documents so messy that I often turned them off just so I could see what I am doing. But – out of sight is out of mind and the ideas can easily get lost when they are invisible. In addition, the format of the comments is uncomfortable to read. By contrast each of the Scrivener fragments I write has metadata attached to it. You can think of metadata as an index card attached to the page containing your writing. Not only can I jot notes, I can record when I wrote it, what state it is in, and give the piece keywords. The keyword function is a form of tagging which allows me to call up similar pieces of writing and read them together.

It's hard to change my mind

I am a 'make a mess and then clean it up' writer. I write, rewrite over it, insert bits, inadvertently repeat myself and change my mind. The simple length of pages in Microsoft Word makes it exhausting for me to write this way because I am always scrolling up and down chasing errant bits of text. Sometimes whole sections have to be moved around. In moments of tiredness accidentally deleting things can be a problem.

Scrivener solves this problem by showing you the fragments as a 'tree' diagram with folders and subfolders. You can easily drag a fragment up and down in the 'tree' to change where it appears in the running order. If you accidentally delete a piece of text (and here is a stroke of pure brilliance) you can fish it out of the trash folder.

Research is not just about words

Research writing involves analysing information, synthesising it and crafting it into new forms. Information appears in the form of words, diagrams, tables and images. Often I want to see these as I write so I can do the analysing and synthesising as I go. Mr Thesis Whisperer recognised my problem awhile back and kindly bought me a second widescreen monitor, which he cleverly rotated to resemble a piece of paper. I write on this screen and have my flotsam on the other. But in Scrivener the miscellaneous 'stuff' I have can be ported directly into the 'research' section of my document, so it is always attached to the project I am working on. Scrivener does the work of remembering which articles or images are pertinent to the piece I am working on and I can use a split screen view to see any of this 'stuff' side by side with my writing. I never print PDFs out and lose them.

Death by Feature

Microsoft Word is old and has been suffering feature creep for some time. There are so many bells and whistles now; I don't know how to operate half of them or even what they are for. The designers of Microsoft Word get credit for the fact that I can still turn out documents without understanding most of the program. My point is that it may well be that everything I am moaning about can be done in Word, but it's hard for me to find out how. There's far fewer buttons in Scrivener; therefore much less to learn. It's a much more restful writing environment, which helps me find the creative headspace I need.

I am not paid to endorse Scrivener (although I wish I was!); there are alternatives out there, some of which are free and open source. It will no doubt amuse you that the guy who designed Scrivener did it to avoid doing his PhD. Now that's some heavy-duty procrastination that I can really get behind.

How to write 1000 words a day (and not go bat shit crazy)

Some years ago, on a plane ride home from a conference, I happened to sit next to a senior academic from my university. This guy is one of those wonderful academics who ~~somehow avoided becoming a grumpy old bastard~~ will still freely talk about his weaknesses to others. One of the things that he told me was not to worry too much about how stupid your ideas look the first time you put them on paper. This was news to me. I had not begun my Thesis Whispering career at that point and was doing my masters degree. I honestly didn't know that pretty much everyone writes a crappy first draft and will rewrite it until it is good. I never rewrote anything as an undergrad and just assumed I was crap at writing academic papers. The charming old guy laughed and said:

"Just remember, there's no such thing as writing: only rewriting"

This line stuck in my head and has become a little mantra I repeat silently to myself as I write a first draft of anything. It brings the sense of near panic under control as my new ideas limp onto the page. In fact, I think half the struggle of a thesis is to get this thinking stuff out of your head and onto the page in order to start the rewriting process. All of us avoid writing sometimes in a vain attempt to avoid confronting the seeming weakness of our ideas. Not writing regularly can have a cost however. When I was nearing the end of my PhD, I added up the number of words I had to write and divided them by the number of days of study leave I had left. Then I freaked out and had to have a little lie down: according to my calculations I had to write 60,000 words in 3 months. After a cup of tea (with maybe just a whiff of scotch in it) I contemplated this problem and made a PLAN, which was cobbled together from all the advice books on writing I used in my workshops with doctoral students. A case of eating my own cooking if you will. This PLAN worked for me and I share it with you here. It works best in the middle to late stages of your PhD, when you have absorbed a lot of information about your topic and have thought about it for a while.

Step one: spend less time at your desk

Now close that Facebook window and listen to Auntie Thesis Whisperer for a moment. The secret to writing at least 1000 words a day is to give yourself a limited time frame in which to do it. What's that I hear you say? "Are you crazy Inger??" Well, as I'm fond of saying to my students, just because Mr or Ms Bottom is paying a trip to Chair Town it does not always follow that productive work is being done. If you give yourself the whole day to write, you will spend the whole day writing and, in the process, drive yourself bat shit crazy. One of my supervisors once said to me: "Doing a thesis is like mucking out a stable". His point was that you have to tackle it one wheelbarrow load of shit at a time. If you stay in the stable too long, the stink will kill you. So dedicate less than a quarter of the day to making some new text and then take a break and return later to clean it up. This sounds counter intuitive, but trust me - it works.

Step Two: remember the two-hour rule

I think most people only have about two really good, creative writing hours in a day. Two hours in which new 'substantive' ideas will make their way onto the page. This is when you must generate the writing that will be rewritten. Most of us are in the best frame of mind for this after breakfast and before lunch - whatever time of the day that happens to be for you. If you sleep until midday and arrive at your office at 3pm after going to the gym it doesn't matter. Writing new stuff should be almost the first thing you do **when you sit down to your desk**. Personally I find it hard to resist the siren call of the email, but if I am on deadline I do an emergency scan then close it until lunchtime.

Step Four: start in the middle

When I am on deadline and need to generate words I don't even attempt to write introductions, conclusions or important transitions. As Howard Becker in his excellent book "Writing for Social Scientists," said: **"How can I introduce it if I haven't written it yet?"** This attitude is echoed in "Helping Doctoral Students to Write", where Kamler and Thomson recommend that thesis writers think about their work in terms of 'chunks' rather than chapters. A chunk can be anything up to two pages long - the text between each subheading if you like. No doubt you have some scrappy notes that you can transcribe or cut into a new file. This acts as a 'seed'. Once you have planted the seed, just start adding on words around and over it - this builds a chunk. Don't worry about where it fits yet - that's a rewriting problem.

Step Four: Write as fast as you can, not as well as you can

This advice also comes from Becker. Thinking happens *during* writing. The surest way to slow the process is to worry too much about whether your thinking is any good. So give yourself permission to write badly. If you can't think of a word use another/ equivalent/filler words: don't slow down and start to think too much. Do this 'free writing' in bursts of about 10 to 15 minutes. When you need a rest, review and fiddle with the text - maybe plant a new seed - then move on to another burst. It's likely you will produce more than 1000 words if you do this for two hours - in fact I usually did around 3000. It's gruelling and bad for your back and shoulders, which is another reason why the two-hour time limit is important.

Step Five: leave it to rest... then re-write

Because you are writing without judgment, most of the words you generate in step four will be crap. Carving off the excess crap in the editing process will reveal the 1000 words of beautiful substantive text you are after. But take a break before you attempt this, or you wont have the necessary perspective. Go and have a coffee with a friend, walk the dog, watch some TV - whatever takes you away from your desk for a couple of hours. Then come back, maybe after dinner, and start sifting through, massaging and editing. Be strategic about this editing - some parts will be easier than others. But do try to pull some 'finished words' - even if it's only a paragraph - back into your draft each day. This gives you a sense of achievement that is important for morale.

The Pomodoro Technique

So that's how I wrote 60,000 words in three months. When I present this method in seminars it invariably horrifies those people who like to write line by perfect line. I'm sympathetic to the reasons people like to write that way, but it seems to me that they suffer a lot more pain than perhaps they need to. Readers of the blog pointed out that the intense writing bursts described above are similar to the 'pomodoro technique' and sent me some links. I read up on it and thought it sounded interesting, but it wasn't until @danya told me about the phone app she used that I tried it out.

I don't know about most of you, but for me the key difficulty in writing productively is staying 'on task' long enough to produce significant amounts of wordage. Inside my screen there are so many potential distractions: Twitter, email, web-surfing, chat, other projects... the list goes on. Not to mention the distractions OUTSIDE of the screen; that work/life balance thing (such as it is)

The pomodoro technique was developed by Francesco Cirillo in the 1980's and is meant to be a way to reduce distraction. The idea is disarmingly simple: just write using a timer and take regular breaks. According to wikipedia (which I am taking as an authority in this instance) there are 5 steps:

1. Decide on the task to be done

2. Set the pomodoro (timer) to 25 minutes
3. Work on the task until the timer rings
4. Take a short break (5 minutes) then do another burst
5. Every four "pomodori" take a longer break (15–20 minutes)

You could use a kitchen timer, but being a techie kind of girl, I took @danya's advice and downloaded the free 'pomodroido' app for my android phone and hoed into a paper with a fast approaching deadline. Within 2 pomodoros of 25 minutes each I had (extremely roughly) put all my ideas down in Scrivener. That put me in a position to start the rewriting process and get it Out The Door. As I did the pomodoros I was struck by the simple brilliance of this technique. The task bar on the pomodroido app advances across the screen and shows you how many minutes you have left. At the end a nice little chime goes off and the phone asks you if you want to take a break or go straight into the next one. I used the 10 minutes to do a quick check of my Twitter and email, then I'd pick a subheading and dive in again.

I noticed I would be able to write for about 12 minutes straight before I looked at the timer. At that point I was feeling itchy and had a strong urge to leave the Scrivener window, but I could see the progress I had made, which somehow made it easier to stay with the feeling and push a bit longer. Like doing squats at the gym in bunches of 10, or a set number of laps of the pool, the physical presence of the timer reminded me that there was an end to the pain soon. During the goofing off in between pomodoros I felt more relaxed than usual. I didn't feel that classic internet emotion which usually sweeps over me while on deadline: a nagging sense of anxiety and guilt undercut with something hard, like desperation.

For those interested in giving it a try who don't own an Android phone here's an iphone equivalent. Those who don't own a smart phone could try downloading one of the numerous PC or Mac applications out there, or even use a free web site if you want. If you visit what I assume is the official pomodoro website there are a few books which build this technique into an overall productivity strategy. But to be honest with you, I think the more complicated a productivity technique becomes the less useful it is. I don't think I'd be comfortable using it for every kind of task, so it wouldn't be a holistic solution to my productivity problems.

This suspicion was confirmed by chatting to a few people on Twitter. @bronwynhinz said while she thought it worked for some kinds of writing, it was less good for other research orientated tasks, like reading or data analysis. While @jasondowns reckons it works for lots of things, like doing transcriptions and 'mind-dumps' (getting words on a page). Jason thinks the pomodoro technique is especially good when you find it hard to start and as a way to limit the time spent doing online journal searches. Everyone is different. You'll have to try it to workout what works for you.

Writing for your readers

Howard Becker once pointed out that writing is first and foremost a social act. Writing for your readers is the most important thing to keep in mind while doing a PhD, but it isn't always easy. @jasondowns helped me understand this difficulty better when he sent me a link to an interview with the writer Tobias Wolff on the subject of writing. Wolff points out that most professional writers tend to be quite boring people because the characteristics that make one a good writer - such as the ability to work alone - are quite anti-social. Many of us do a PhD because we like to teach; teaching is profession where you talk for a living. By contrast writers spend most of their time in their own heads struggling with their own ideas. If you are a social person by inclination it's not surprising it can be a struggle to write for long periods of time.

The anti social nature of writing as a process - at least when you aren't doing it as part of a shut up and write group! - explains why we can be so easily distracted. Wolff says simply: "All I need is a window to not write". How true this is - for me at least. In fact, over the holidays I found myself starting to clean the fridge just to avoid going back to the keyboard. This is one of the reasons why regular habits are the writer's friend.

I started the Thesis Whisperer blog in July 2010. For some time I had been vaguely wanting to write down some thoughts on the topic of doing a thesis - both from my own experience and from my work with PhD students at RMIT. But I lacked a format that was going to encourage me to write. Writing into a word document felt like writing a thesis again - and I was so, so over that. Writing a blog feels more like you are talking to someone, not just putting words on a page. As soon as you hit 'publish' your words are out there. Delightfully, people write back in the comments section and let you know what they think.

Blogging feels more like a social act than a writing act. Maybe in here is a little insight that can help with the writing of a thesis. If you are struggling with the unsocial nature of the writing process it helps to bring your audience into sharper focus. Since your most important audience is your examiners, one thing I recommend all students do sometime in second year is to write an examiner profile. This is easy for you students in the USA as you will already know your panel, but for people in the UK and Australasia the examiners are outsiders who will not have seen the thesis before. You will have to imagine them, so why not use some techniques from fiction writers? A writer might use a series of questions to 'sketch' their character in words. Here's a list to get you going:

Write a one sentence summary describing your examiner's academic 'flavour'
What sort of things does my examiner already know about my topic?

What is my examiner interested in theoretically?
What methods does my examiner like to use?
What might my examiner expect to learn from reading this thesis?
What annoys my examiner?

This little exercise will help you form a 'picture' of your examiner in your head as you write. I encourage you to show such a list to your supervisor to make sure that you both are on the same page about who will be reading the work when it is done. Once you have spent a bit of time developing up this 'examiner' you can then imagine them sitting by your side, reading the page you are drafting. I think it's perfectly ok to talk to your examiner in your head:

What do you think of that last sentence? Do you agree with that idea? No? Maybe I need to fill you in on a little more theory?

Despite your efforts to imagine the audience, a thesis can be a difficult document to write, as there are multiple potential audiences: your examiners, your supervisors and a professional audience that may or may not be composed of academics. A while back I received an email from @thetokenlefty, which summed up the difficulty of writing for multiple audiences:

I had a quick question for you about this 5,000-word literature review I have to write for my methods course.

It is going to be read and marked by people like yourself -- not engineers, much less engineers in the narrow area I will be writing in.

The simple question I have is: should I write this lit review for the audience marking it, or write it as if it were a real part of my thesis? That is, assuming a very high level of understanding by the reader.

This question really pertains to writing my thesis as well. I'm finding it hard to strike a balance. I am used to my academic writing being used to demonstrate my understanding, which runs the risk of insulting/boring a thesis examiner!

@thetokenlefty is right to worry in this way. In their excellent book "Helping Doctoral Students to write" Kamler and Thomson explain how talking down to your reader (boring them witless with basic information they already know) or assuming they know more than they do (loading your thesis with obscure ideas and language) are two basic mistakes that many thesis writers make. Kamler and Thompson claim that thesis writers face the 'Goldilocks dilemma'. The content and style of the thesis should be not too hot, not too cold, but just right.

Mullins and Kiley argue a similar line in their seminal paper: "It's a PhD, not a Nobel prize" where they explore how examiners examine theses, specifically how they decide whether it is good or not. One of the things the examiners Mullins and Kiley interviewed said was that they want to *learn* something new from reading your thesis. This tells us that a thesis is more than a show of erudition; it must inform and explain at the same time as showing off your scholarly abilities.

The work of the thesis writer is therefore twofold: finding out *what* you need to say and working out *how* do you need to say it. However this twofold task is complicated by the fact that many students will have @thetokenlefty's problem: how do you do this for multiple audiences in one document?

I would suggest that you start by doing a basic audience analysis. During an excellent talk on writing for exhibitions I attended, some people from Melbourne Museum explained how they researched their audiences and represented them as a matrix. The idea was that every museum patron sits somewhere in this Cartesian grid:

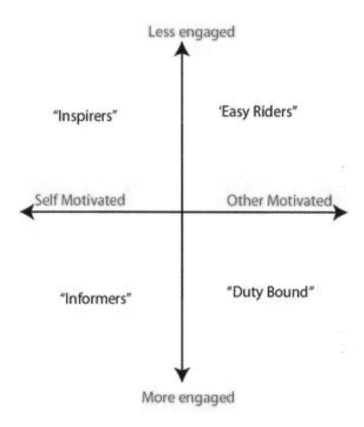

The 'easy riders' are parents out to amuse the kids on a Saturday afternoon. Easy riders are less engaged (ie: not as into finding out information) as the 'duty bound' parents, who were taking their kids to the museum as an educational activity.

However both sets of parents were 'other motivated', ie: visiting for their kids rather than themselves. The 'self motivated' museum visitors occupy the left hand side of the matrix. The 'inspirers' come to openings, but are less engaged in the museum content than the 'informers' who were there for the purposes of educating themselves.

Of course, some Easy riders will be more engaged than others and some informers not as interested in learning, but I think this diagram is a useful simplification nonetheless. The exhibition designers told us that they target their shows at one or two audience types only, but they make sure there is a mix of different exhibitions so there is always something at the museum for everyone. Clever.

I am going to use this idea of identifying, targeting and accommodating specific audiences for @tokenleftys thesis in a diagram, which hopefully can be applied to yours as well. First I have identified 4 potential audiences for @thetokenlefty's work:

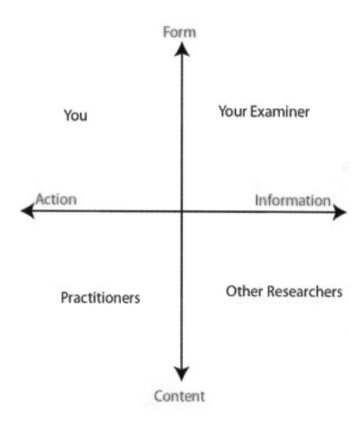

@thetokenlefty as the writer, his examiners, practitioners (in this case professional solar energy engineers) and other researchers in the area of engineering and solar power generation.

Now @thetokenlefty and his examiner are probably more concerned with the form of the thesis: is it coherent? Do all the chapters follow on from each other? Have all the questions been answered? Other researchers might be reading for specific content. They probably wont read the whole thing from start to finish but will dip in and out to find the things they need.

Practicing engineers will be similar to researchers, but they may need more background as they will not be as immersed in the literature. Hopefully practitioners will be looking to take action on the information contained in the thesis @thetokenlefty's work. I have put 'research' on the opposing axis to 'action' because I think examiners and other researchers will be interested in generating research based on things they find in the thesis.

What advice can we give @thetokenlefty based on this analysis?

He needs first and foremost how to cater to the needs of each different audience: what does each audience know already? and What do they want to learn about? An examiner will know different things to a practitioner, who in turn will be looking for different things to a post doc.

The challenge for @thetokenlefty is how to make the ideas and content which is relevant to each audience *accessible.* For example, @thetokenlefty may want to have more 'simple' information that is necessary to a practitioner alongside, but not in, the main text so it doesn't bore the examiner and other researchers. He might put this basic information in footnotes or an appendix, but there are other ways: a common magazine trick is to use easy to read panels alongside the text.

There are other ideas, but no more room! So I will leave you with this thought: who are your audiences and how might you re-purpose - or redraw - this diagram for them?

Dealing with procrastination

I have come to the conclusion there is no one sure for procrastination, just a series of tactics. Everyone is a candidate for procrastination woes, you don't have be doing a thesis to suffer from them. For example, in 2010 I put out two papers to top journals containing my thesis results from 2009. Both editors wanted to publish, but asked for significant changes. I found the process of revisiting these articles incredibly hard work and never did manage to get them in. It would be fair to say that Procrastination Fairy sprinkled me with her Can't Be Bothered dust in a big way. The revision the editors were asking for felt like a profoundly unpleasant activity. The problem with a peer review, if properly applied, is that it leads to DOUBT. To some extent I have lost confidence in the work and started to second-guess myself. As a consequence, the whole time I had the documents open I had an uncomfortable sense of failure. It became easy - far too easy - just not to open the documents in the first place.

There's lots of advice out there on the subject of procrastination - in fact one of the nicest forms of procrastination in my opinion is reading the advice. It was while doing this that I came across a great article on procrastination in the New Yorker by James Surowieki an extended review on an academic book on the topic of procrastination called _"The thief of time". Surowiecki uses the work in this book to argue that procrastination can be seen as the "quintessential modern problem". Academics, Surowiecki claims, are particularly prone to procrastination, perhaps because of the largely self-directed nature of their work. I'm not sure this is the only reason, but procrastination is certainly the key lament I hear in my work-shops with PhD students and at pleasantly procrastinaterly coffees with colleagues.

The problem with procrastination is that it doesn't help much to tell yourself that procrastination is a stupid thing to do. We all know that the unpleasant sensations that arise from putting off an unpleasant (or boring) task can be as bad, even worse, than actually doing the task you avoiding in the first place. So what to do? Well, a couple of lines in Surowiecki's article jumped out at me for suggesting a way forward, the first one was this:

"... procrastinators are self-handicappers: rather than risk failure, they prefer to create conditions that make success impossible"

Ouch! Maybe that one is a little too close to the bone... A more fruitful line of attack was suggested in this quote:

"... when we put off preparing for that meeting by telling ourselves that we'll do it tomorrow, we fail to take into account that tomorrow the temptation to put off work will be just as strong."

This precisely explained my problem with revising the papers. Every day I told myself that I will start that revision tomorrow, and when tomorrow came the urge to delay was as strong as ever. When my dilemma is put this way the answer is obvious - I need outside pressure to counteract the inner urge to put off the job. I suppose this is why the imposition of deadlines on PhD students is ultimately a good thing. You don't have to defer the responsibility to your institution either; creating your own deadlines within candidature and agreeing on them with your supervisors is good strategy for overcoming the urge to delay writing. A deadline is not the only kind of outside pressure available to you: living on a student income gets pretty intolerable after a couple of years. Many students give finances as a reason they were finally able to hand their thesis in.

Deadlines are not the whole solution of course. The curious nature of procrastination was captured well in in another line from Surowiecki's article:

"... we often procrastinate not by doing fun tasks but by doing jobs whose only allure is that they aren't what we should be doing"

The truth of this struck deeply. I often do research that involves reading policy documents from every other university and putting their key points in a matrix. A more excruciatingly boring research task I can barely think of - yet I would happily do it rather than open and start revising those damn papers. Maybe the way to overcome this is to focus more on the feelings about the work - not just on the rational reasons why the work must be done. Personally I need a way to start feeling a sense of anticipation, instead of dread; a way to ignite that spark of interest and curiosity in the work itself so I *want* to open those files.

Visualising can help here. I could try closing my eyes and imagining that elusive state of 'flow', the state of being at one with the work of writing, which is pleasurable in and of itself. I could try to summon up the glow of accomplishment I will feel when the job is finished... nope - that's not working either.

The final thought of Surowiecki's I want to share is, I think, the most powerful of all: procrastination may stem from the nature of identity. We are not, as we would like to believe, unified selves, but "different beings, jostling, contending, and bargaining for control" within one body.

Our 'multiple selves' want different things. My 'want to get published in an A* journal' self is in constant struggle with my other selves: my 'want to have coffee', 'want to read twitter', 'want to write for the blog', and my 'want to empty my email inbox' selves - just to name a few.

To my mind this explanation makes perfect sense. My 'want to get published in an A* self' will always be at a disadvantage compared those selves who have more intrinsically interesting - and easy to satisfy - desires. The trick then is to think of what kind of bargain I can make with my 'want to have coffee' self that will enable me to open those files...While you think about that I might go and have a coffee.

Getting it out the door

I don't know about you, but I love the editing stage because it means my article or chapter is nearly done and I will shortly have another achievement to list on my CV. I know that sounds boringly pragmatic and instrumental, but there it is. While I have a deep love of scholarship and a healthy interest in ideas, my urge to write is driven by an interest in career maintenance - pure and simple.

In his superb book "Writing for social scientists" (which should be renamed "Writing for everyone"), Howard Becker talks about the importance of being the kind of writer who can get stuff "Out The Door". He suggests writers need to think more like companies who make gadgets like phones and computers. Electronic consumer goods companies have similar problems to writers, but they have shipping schedules they must stick to if they want to stay in business.

The engineers will want to delay shipping until the product matches the vision in their heads, but the marketing people will be happy with 'good enough'. Even if the new gadget is rough around the edges, the marketing people will still make the engineers get it Out The Door. According to Becker the logic of the marketing people is simple: if it sells, there will be money for to build the next version. The next version is likely to be better, but, meanwhile, this one will do.

Your success at getting your writing Out The Door will be affected by your temperament as a researcher. If you are the kind of researcher who has a curiosity problem, as I mentioned earlier in this book, your ability to get it Out The Door can be hampered by a tendency to get bored. I have a friend who struggled mightily with her Masters degree because she hated working over what she called 'cold cases' - her chapter drafts. Once the ideas were on paper she claimed her curiosity had been satisfied and she was ready to move on. This is where your marketing department needs to call you in for a performance review: that attitude is not going to shift enough product to keep the company afloat.

Sometimes however, boredom is not the dark side of a creative turn of mind, but a lack of commitment to seeing the idea through. Just like the idea of having a baby is different from the reality of wiping its bottom 6 times a day, thinking about ideas is a lot less work than writing about them. The problem with intellectual labour is, although it can be hard, the effects of the struggle are not visible.

My favourite scene in the sitcom "Big Bang Theory" is where two of the characters, Sheldon and Raj, are collaborating on a physics problem. The scene consists of jump cuts of the two scientists, staring at equations on a whiteboard, while "Eye of the Tiger", the theme music to the movie 'Rocky', plays. The scene perfectly captures the inner experience of intellectual struggle vs the outer appearance of ... well, pretty much nothing.

For all our labouring in the footnote salt mines, there will be no callouses on our hands, so it can be hard to see your commitment problem for what it really is: work avoidance. If you realise your will is flagging, your inner marketing department has to call in pizza for the engineering department and get them doing overtime. Promise yourself a reward for completion - chocolate, TV, a walk in the park - whatever it takes to keep Mr or Ms Bottom in chair town long enough to get it Out The Door. If you couple a lack of commitment with a tendency to excessive self-critique you will be in real trouble.

I have seen some of the brightest people fail to get a PhD because they measure their efforts against the best The Literature has to offer. Unfortunately the best work is often written by academics with years and years of experience of their craft. No matter how hard you try; you will never catch up with them. These are the people most likely to fall victim to the seductive whispering of the inner engineering department: "Just one more week and it will be perfect - we promise". This is when your marketing department needs to step in, take the project out of your hands and ship the bastard anyway.

For some lucky people doing a PhD is an intellectual luxury, but for most of us plebs it isn't. Many of you will soon be out there with a newly minted PhD looking for work; some of you will be there already. We can rail against the quality and quantity metrics that dominate academia as much as we like, but they are a fact of life for now. In my opinion it's only going to become increasingly competitive. As Becker points out: people will judge you on what you have done - not the ideas you have in your head. Finished theses, chapters and journal articles are the only tangible proof of your invisible labours in the footnote mines.

So remember: your inner engineering department does not always have your best interests at heart. You may not like your inner marketing department, but when they do their job properly you won't go broke. Repeat after me: "Perfect is the enemy of Done".

Reducing your word count

In 2011 I got my first taste of helping Thesis Whisperer Jnr, aged nine and a half, with an essay for school. I had been looking forward to this moment because, to be frank, I'd been pretty useless as a homework helper up to that moment. I have long since forgotten all my long division and have only the vaguest grip on biology. Since I supervise PhD students and write this blog for a living I was calmly confident that I could be a primary school writing tutor in my sleep.

Boy, was I wrong.

It took us nearly 6 hours to write around 500 words and by the end of it we were screaming at each other. Mr Thesis Whisperer eventually had to step in and break up the fight with some stern words, luckily mostly directed at Thesis Whisperer Jnr ("Listen to your mother son - she has a PhD, you don't"). We fought because we had fundamentally opposing positions on how writing should be done.

Thesis Whisperer Jnr objected strongly to changing anything once it was written. While he wanted to get the job done as quickly as possible, I wanted to linger over the details. For me the first draft is just a starting point for further work. This episode made me think about how difficult it is to learn how to be edited (and that primary school teachers have a much harder job than I do!).

I have come to view the big red editing pen as a tool of kindness. For this reason I am equally brutal with the red pen when I am asked to edit other people's work. Thesis Whisperer Jnr could not cope with this approach and he is not alone. People often react with shock to my editing style; perhaps because I am generally mild mannered in person and my vicious red pen seems out of character. I understand how they feel. While I mostly enjoy the process of editing my own work, I still find it painful. Losing words you have carefully crafted hurts. I still have trouble accepting uncomplimentary peer reviews. Although I recognise the value of letting other people into my work, at some primitive level I just resent being criticised. But I have learned to swallow my pride and accept it (or at least fake a good natured acceptance, while continuing to seethe inside).

There is a strong emotional component bundled up in the act of writing and I think Elizabeth Kubler-Ross's 5-stage model of grief is a good way to think about it. Kubler Ross interviewed people who were dealing with a terminal illness in order to better understand the (Western) culture around death. Her five stages of grief describes the process of dealing with death and dying: Denial, Anger, Bargaining, Depression and finally, Acceptance. These feelings are not necessarily sequential - it doesn't always follow that you will get to acceptance straight after depression. This is especially true when you apply this concept to writing; you may jump around these feelings, or even be in two states at the same time. Let's dwell on each emotion for a moment.

Denial is a trap that is easy to fall into. It can be emotionally easier to stay in Denial about the quality of our writing rather than work to improve it. Part of this is a fear of criticism, which can manifest in resistance to showing your work to others before it is 'perfect'. Writing is part of the way we express ourselves; criticism of our writing ability is often taken to be criticism about our thinking ability.

Anger is a common emotion to this perceived criticism of the self. Facing up to feelings of failure or inadequacy is confronting, especially when we are adults. Sometimes Anger is directed at ourselves because, in retrospect, writing those lost words seems like a waste of time. Occasionally the Anger is directed at others, like the anonymous peer reviewer, or your supervisor.

It can be particularly galling to be asked to take something out of your thesis that the supervisor suggested should be there in the first place. When you are Angry it is easy to see this kind of supervisor behaviour as capricious. It takes an effort of will to put yourself in their place and realise that they can't always predict if something is a good idea until they see it on paper.

When the Anger cools off we may slip into Bargaining in the vain hope of avoiding making changes.

Sometimes supervision meetings can turn into unproductive bargaining sessions, especially when student and supervisor disagree. My PhD supervisor realised early on that a chapter I had planned was just not going to be feasible, and told me so. It took me a year or so to accept this and I wasted meeting time trying to convince him that he was wrong.

In my experience the *idea* of losing words is often more Depressing than the reality. When I have bitten the bullet and done a good hard edit I usually feel a sense of accomplishment, but contemplating that task can induce lethargy and procrastination.

Ultimately I think we need to work towards inhabiting Kubler Ross's final stage - Acceptance. Acceptance is when you stop caring about your writer's ego as much and can be more open to suggested changes. When you have managed to internalise this state of mind you can critically evaluate any suggestions for improvement on their own merit, not merely react to them emotionally.

Next time I have to help Thesis Whisperer with an essay I am going to try to have more patience. At 40 I am still striving to conquer the feelings aroused by the editing process and I suspect that it might take me a lifetime to do it with grace. It's unreasonable of me to expect a 9 year old to be more mature. We all need to go easy and reflect on our feelings in order to process them in a way that helps, rather than hinders our progress towards this goal.

Once you have got over yourself with respect to requested revisions and the process of being edited by your supervisor you may find yourself holding a knife - a virtual one of course. I'm talking about the process of cutting words out of your thesis or dissertation text. Many PhD students may have trouble imagining they can reach, let alone exceed, the magic 90,000 word count (which is the maximum our university allows). Yet, by the end, almost everyone has war stories about having to lose large portions of text: "I got to 120,000 words and my supervisor told me to lose 40,000! That's a whole Masters thesis!"

Usually there are two main reasons you have to cut:

To match a specified word count and/or

Remove text that no longer 'fits' because the direction or focus of the PhD has changed.

Cutting words becomes more difficult as the thesis gets longer; things you say in one place start to affect things you say in other places. You may set out with good intentions, determined to slash and burn your text in an attempt to reduce the overall word count, yet it is quite possible to *increase* that word count by the time you are done 'fixing'. Many professional writers say that developing an ability to know what has to be thrown away is necessary to becoming a good writer. The notorious sci-fi writer Harlan Ellison said that a writer should throw out the first million words. His claim was that it's only after you have written this much that you start to get good. I don't think thesis writers should take this seriously as it might lead to dark, nihilistic thoughts which are the enemy of Done. A good thesis is a finished thesis, but it still needs to be chock full of wordy goodness.

Those sentences that we love the most can be the hardest to do away with. For me it's sentences that exhibit a particularly nifty turn of phrase, usually some kind of pun, which are hard to cut. I cling to them tenaciously, despite the fact that they are making my writing "flippant" (as my PhD supervisor put it once. Ouch.)

When holding the proverbial knife, it is good to remind yourself that the text is better off without these words, or as Stephen King put it more colourfully:

"... kill your darlings, kill your darlings, even when it breaks your egocentric little scribbler's heart, kill your darlings."

That quote is from King's excellent book "On Writing" by the way, which I recommend you hunt out and read sometime, but don't leave off your reading on global terrorism or particle physics for goodness sake. On the premise that these successful writers should know a thing or two about the craft, here are 5 ways to kill your darlings:

Use that strike through tool

You know - the one that ~~does this neat thing~~.
Back in the day, way before word processors were
invented, we used to be pretty good at the old strike
through for dealing bits of text that weren't quite right.
Then someone invented liquid paper and it was downhill
from there. The strike through function enables you to
keep the text where it was and use it as a reference as
you write around it. You can always un-strike through if
you decide the original was better and you're right back
where you started, no harm no foul as they say.

Move the questionable text to the footnotes

This technique works on the principle of out of
sight, out of mind. The footnotes give you a place to let
the words go gently into that good night as the poet
Dylan Thomas once said. By the time you come to your
final polish you are usually in the position to pull the
trigger and kill those darlings because the words clearly
aren't needed anymore.

Start a 'maybe later' folder

I got this tip from Dr Alex Selenitsch. When Alex
was doing his PhD he kept having many ideas that
weren't right for his thesis, but were still good. He would
cut and paste them into a new document and stash the
excess words into his 'maybe later' folder. I started one of

these myself, years ago, but have yet to dip into it and resurrect any of the bits of writing stashed there. My 'maybe later' folder is a bit like the footnotes: an ideas graveyard where unwanted text can rest in peace.

Triage your text

Brent Allpress at RMIT gave me this idea when I was doing my Masters degree. Go through your text and put a number against each paragraph: 1, 2 and 3. Keep all the 1's, throw out all the 3s and try to cut the 2's in half. I found this works only on short sections of text between subheads, but it is highly effective when preparing journal papers.

Perform bypass surgery

A good thesis is a tightly integrated text - all the various parts rely on each other to a greater or lesser extent. In this sense your text is like your body: you will probably die if someone took out your lungs, whereas you can probably stand to lose your leg (no pun intended :-). Sometimes taking out a whole chapter or section makes more sense than trying to nip little bits out from all over the place. You can always think about moving the dead bit of text to the appendix (again - no pun intended. Maybe).

How to de-clutter your writing

Earlier this year I found myself in a bookstore with a $100 book voucher burning a hole in my pocket, when I spied a book called 'On writing well: the classic guide to writing non fiction' by William Zinsser. According to the cover 'On writing well' has sold more than a million copies, which piqued my curiosity (just as the publisher had intended). Since book vouchers are like academic candy - impossible not to spend instantly - I bought it straight away.

I am a sucker for any book on writing. I thought I already owned everything worthy in the genre, but clearly not. The difference between Zinsser's book and many others is that it deals with technicalities at the same time as being an inspiring call to action. Zinsser is all about the audience and how to make their reading experience more enjoyable without dumbing down your text - something all thesis writers must be interested in. I encourage you to go right out and buy this book if you don't own it already.

To convince you further here's 5 ways to de-clutter your text based on some of Zinsser's ideas.

Use brackets to diagnose 'fuzz' in your text

All writers (will have to) edit their prose, but (the) great writers edit (it) viciously, always trying to eliminate (words which are) 'fuzz' - (excess) words (which are not adding anything of value). Zinsser compares (the process of editing out) 'fuzz' to fighting weeds - you will always be slightly behind (because they creep in when you aren't looking for them). One of my (pet hates) is (the word) 'also'. (If you search and replace all instances (of this word) you will find you can live without it and your writing will improve (instantly). (Likewise the word)'very'.)

Let's try that again:

All writers edit their prose, but great writers edit viciously. The point of editing is to eliminate 'fuzz', or excess words which don't add value. Zinsser compares removing 'fuzz' to fighting weeds - you will always be slightly behind. Two examples of fuzz are 'also' and 'very'. Work at keeping them out of your text and your writing will improve.

Pay attention to your adverbs and such

I'm a child of the 70's, when, it seems, they gave up teaching grammar. I can't explain what an adverb is, but I know one when I see it. Zinsser points out that "smile happily" doesn't say much more than "smile" and that the tall in "tall skyscraper" is redundant. If you start to mentally put brackets around these words as you read you will start to see adverb abuse everywhere - which unfortunately makes reading trashy novels (very) irritating.

Get rid of qualifiers

Zinsser claims that qualifiers "weaken any sentence they inhabit". Phrases like "in a sense", "a bit", "sort of" have no place in a thesis. Worse - they imply that you are apologetic or unsure of your ideas. This is not a message you want to send to your examiners.

Strive for nuance

Grammar hurts my brain. It's like trying to understand how I am walking *as* I walk and makes me dizzy. So I will make this next point without resorting to technical explanations. This advice comes out of Chapter 7 of Kamler and Thomson's excellent book "Helping doctoral students to write", but I think Zinsser would have approved. Consider the following sentences:

Inger *argues* that the words you use to describe the work of others is important

Inger *asserts* that the words you use to describe the work of others is important

Inger *states* that the words you use to describe the work

of others is important

Inger *outlines* that the words you use to describe the work of others is important

There's quite a difference between 'argues' and 'asserts'. The first implies that Inger is making a case; the second implies that Inger is defending a position without necessarily providing any evidence for it. 'Asserts' adds a whiff of arrogance, but without over playing it (remember that academia is in a state of polite warfare). Likewise 'stating' something is different from 'outlining' it - the latter implies that some explanation is supplied which will help the reader understand what is being discussed. Paying attention to the words you use to describe the work of others saves you the trouble of adding another sentence to explain to the reader what *you* think of the work. It's the thesis writer's equivalent of a nod and a wink to the reader. It's hard work to remember all that nuance, so I keep a handy list of verbs on my wall.

Prune

It's hard to write well on a subject if you don't understand it clearly. Sometimes the only way to get to the idea is to write it out. It's likely that you will generate far more text than you can, or should, use. It can be tempting to 'dress up' your writing to appear more intelligent. Resist the urge. The ideas and findings in a thesis are important; style is secondary. A simple and precise style is like painting your walls white - a backdrop against which your ideas can pop. It can be hard to do the necessary pruning, but remember that examiners are likely to view a thinner thesis as a sign that you are confident and in charge of your material.

Knowing when to 'stop'

PhD students are resourceful people - sometimes all they need is a pep talk and they end up solving any given problem themselves. One of the pep talks in my repertoire is the "It's Time" talk. By this I mean - it's time to have that difficult conversation with your supervisor about scholarly independence. Let me explain.

In my time as a research educator I have had discussions with quite a few students who were arguing with their supervisors (panel members if you are studying in the USA) about whether or not the PhD was ready for examination. All these students, I might add, were physically and emotionally exhausted. Some were in tears as they me they just couldn't carry on. These students have extreme reactions to a problem that confronts all research students: how to become a fully independent scholar.

Now when I started the Thesis Whisperer blog I promised myself I would be careful about how I approach the issues around student / supervisor relationships. It's a particularly fraught area. If you don't believe me just do a Google search on the term "I hate my supervisor" and see how many hits you get. One of the reasons that the relationships can be so fraught is that there's a paradox at the heart of research supervision. The stated intent of the PhD process is to train novices to become 'independent scholars'. Further, these are novice scholars are supposed to be engaged in making 'new knowledge'. This puts all supervisors in a difficult position.

There should come a point, sooner or later in this process, where the student knows more than the supervisor about your topic. If you think about it - this is in the finest tradition of teaching. The great privilege of research supervision is that a teacher gets to step back knowing that the student has surpassed them and will go on to do Great Things. If the process has worked *you* will be in the best position to judge the quality of your work and be able to tell your supervisor it is ready - and they will agree. The supervisor has helped you to develop what they already have - an internal critic. This internal critic you have formed while doing a PhD will be your friend for life - it is the essence of scholarly independence and will enable you to do the job of an academic.

A caveat. Your thesis being 'ready' does not mean that it is perfect. Perfect is, as my dear husband says, the enemy of Good. Perfect is also the enemy of Done.

Of course, if your supervisor's internal critic and your internal critic disagree everything should come to a screaming halt. The supervisors I meet take their responsibility for overseeing student welfare extremely seriously. Heck – you might even count them as a friend by this point. Although the supervisor may give many reasons for withholding their permission to submit, it usually boils down to one: they see flaws in your work that make them think this will happen and don't want you to fail or have a horrible year of making substantial revisions.

This is why I advise students to swallow their pride and make the revisions that are being asked for. However some of the tearful students reject this advice. Some have already accepted the possibility of revisions or failure and tell me they would rather take a chance on examination (this is in the Australian and UK system of course, where examiners are at arms length from the candidate). Other students violently disagreed with the changes being suggested by the supervisor, arguing the thesis would be worse if they made them. Part of my 'It's Time' pep talk is to point out the paradoxical nature of research supervision and the complex issue of scholarly independence.

Developing empathy with the supervisor, rather than seeing them as the problem, enables you to go back and have an honest conversation about the risks you are prepared to take. Supervisors can be relieved to hear that you are willing take responsibility for the work and its flaws. Often this is enough for the examination process to begin. In rare cases however the It's Time talk doesn't work. If you profoundly disagree with your supervisor about the final changes, perhaps a second opinion is called for. It surprises me how often students think they can't ask for another person to read the thesis when they are in this situation. Hopefully you have a second supervisor or another person in the department who can act as a circuit breaker.

It's best to try to negotiate with your supervisor about who this third reader will be so that you can both be comfortable with their advice. You will need to be prepared for this person to tell you to put your ego back on the shelf and make the changes, because, I'm sorry to tell you - this is what usually happens. Remember: you might be stubborn rather than right.

So - in the end there are no easy answers. I can only highlight the complexity of the issue and encourage honest communication.

PhD detachment

A little while ago @soilduck asked me on Twitter:

"What are some strategies people have used to get through last 6 months of #phd? Emotionally etc ... I just realised I have t-minus 6 months (exactly) until my thesis is due... Was thinking of practical things to help people regardless of situation?"

I don't have all the answers, so I asked on Twitter for suggestions for such a post and many people chimed in with advice. Some took up the theme of general craziness of end times; @julianhopkins quipped "last 6 months? Am in it... do people survive it?" @fiona_rachel confessed, "I've got 4 months left and I'm listening to a lot of country music. Is this normal?" to which @JanetFulton replied "I've got about 8 weeks to go and I'm reading The Bobbsey Twins so country music sounds pretty normal to me".

Others had very practical suggestions about managing your life through this period, such as @julialeventon who warned people not to try anything new, like moving house or learning a language. She also suggested "a regular day off where you don't turn on your computer" (which sounded like a great idea to me). @danya suggested that you "Resist the temptation to get more articles and rerun analysis"; counseling that you need to learn to "accept less than perfect and move on" and our regular supervision correspondent @sarahthesheepu wisely advised: "don't panic, just write and, most importantly read all the regulations about submitting". The most surprising contribution of this sort was from @sharmanedit who told me she had continued with volunteer work. She claimed that doing work for others reminded her not to get too insular. This seems like a neat solution to the almost inevitable selfishness that can manifest under thesis pressure and puts pressure on relationships.

Many mentioned the importance of food and beverages in the writing process, such as @peatyg who found herself: "eating lots of ice-cream, which I never liked b4" (a problem to which I could relate). @tassie_gal suggested: "coffee - lots of. Chocolate - double the amount you think you need"; advice which was taken a step further by @TheEndeavour who suggested "guarana tablets over coffee for those looking for extra study energy" (She did add that you should always check dosage guidelines!). The best one was, from @kiriwhan: "At a rate of 0.75L of Pepsi Max per 1000 words, I'm going to need 60L to finish my thesis..." which I thought combined the time line and food advice nicely.

Amongst all this practical advice @boredpostdoc said: "I probably could have applied for an extension, but by that point I just wanted out". I could relate to this, I clearly remember there was a point where I stopped caring whether what I was doing a good job or not and just wanted out. I felt like I was **in** a bad marriage with this alien thing, which was no longer bringing me any joy. These sentiments are echoed in a very funny Open Letter on the Mc Sweeney website, which reads like a break up note written by a student to their thesis:

"I am tired of people asking about you: they always ask about you, how you're doing, how far I've gone with you. To be honest, I want to see this through to the end, I want to go all the way with you, but then I want to put this relationship behind me."

Clearly this detachment thing is a bonafide #phdemotion. This made me wonder, why is 'detachment' so necessary to completion? In western knowledge cultures (a fancy way of saying the world of scholarship which you live in, right now) we tend to promote an attitude of attachment - to ideas, our writing, our thoughts. In fact the whole of academia is built on ownership of ideas - hence all the fretting over issues like plagiarism. Ownership is very important to the process of making a thesis, which is why some of those who have very dominating supervisors can find the process a struggle. I believe a sense of ownership is necessary; it helps us fight the battles we face with supervisors, with spouses, with university guidelines and all the rest of (what feels like) an uncaring world who just get in the way of finishing the damn thesis.

But I wonder if perhaps, at a certain point, this

sense of ownership just gets in the way and it is better to strive for a state of detachment. I mean Detachment in the Buddhist sense, which doesn't have the same kind of negative connotations as it usually does in English. Now I am only an interested dabbler in Buddhism, but as I understand it the problem with attachment is that it leads to craving, and craving can lead to pain. For example, when we cling too tightly to people in relationships, it can lead us to craving their presence. A fear of losing the person can lead us to act in ways that are harmful to others, as well as ourselves (you only have to go through one bad relationship break up to feel the truth of this insight).

Many of us do a thesis for the status and recognition it is meant to bring - and the employment opportunities we hope it will enable. But this craving can provoke a fear of failure - which can be crippling. The fear of failing can lead us into the valley of perfectionism. The best way to detach yourself from this fear, I believe, is to understand the examination process as one which will make the thesis better, not a pass/fail proposition. In any case, the university wont let you hang around forever so taking an active part in detaching yourself when the time comes is probably for the best.

Presenting your research for review or Viva

Presentations to a faculty or disciplinary audience are subtly different to those you give at a conference, but not talked about as often. These internal presentations are important because they tell your colleagues what kind of researcher you are; it helps you socially and academically to perform well to your peers. Many research students must complete a Viva, or verbal examination, towards the end of their degree. In my role as a research educator I have sat in on many of these as well as completion seminars and confirmations. Before that I sat through literally hundreds of assessment presentations if you count my years in ~~purgatory~~ architecture school. So here's my top five classic research presentation mistakes, but I'm going to stick with the verbal problems here because there are many great presentations about graphics out there on the web.

TMI

Too much information (TMI) is the most common mistake I see and one I have indulged in a few times myself. I see it most often in completion seminars where the student has a full draft and can no longer see the forest for the trees. You know that you are heading for TMI when you start to feel like you are drowning in facts and figures that don't seem to relate to each other. You know you have a case of TMI in front of you when the presentation is full of tangents, where the student veers off course to explain, often in painful detail, definitions, counter arguments, collection problems and the like. It's frustrating to listen to because you feel like the student is never going to get to the point. By the time they actually do, you have lost interest and started thinking earnestly about lunch. A presentation like this is unlikely to make you look like a lightweight, but it can make you look more confused than you are.

All theory, no action

It's a difficult line to walk with theory sometimes. Not enough can make your project look lightweight; too much can make it look like you spent 4 years gazing at your navel and not *doing* anything. Recently I watched a creative research viva, which involved some design work along with a theoretical 'exegesis'. The student spent the majority of her presentation explaining the theory behind practice based research in exquisite detail; in fact she did rather a good job of this, but she didn't leave enough time to talk about her project work. It must have seemed like a good strategy because her examiners were not from the design research field, unfortunately these people had already read her text, which went through much of the same explanation, and the rest of the audience were designers – who already knew the arguments. Instead of reassuring the examiners that her research approach was legitimate, the second lengthy exposition gave the perverse impression that the student was defensive and unsure of herself. I think it's best to keep explanations of theory short and precise, but tell the audience you are happy to address it during question time. It makes you look smarter if you can answer theoretical questions on your feet anyway.

Why are we here?

Sometimes students race through an explanation of data without enough lead in for me to understand what the problem was in the first place. Without an explanation – however cursory – of the bigger world in which the research is situated I cannot understand fully why the research matters. A more troubling manifestation of the 'why are we here?' problem is when the student that doesn't tell us what the research means at the end of it – data and interpretations are offered but there's no sense of what might come next, what use the research could be or how it changes anything in that bigger world beyond the thesis. Maybe it's just me, but I like to see that the researcher has some questions remaining, or that there were extra questions raised by doing the research in the first place. Perhaps people leave these out in an effort to make the research seem 'finished' or 'under control'? I'm not sure – but please tell me why I am here because otherwise I could be doing my own work and I will come away from your presentation feeling cranky.

Undigested text

Oh boy – where do I start with this one? Reading straight from your paper or thesis is almost always a mistake. Most academic text is not, as they say in the music industry a 'radio friendly unit shifter'. We all know that what sounds delightfully erudite on the page can come across as pompous out loud… but it's a trap which so many of us fall into again and again. I'm as guilty as the next person of reading out chunks of written text rather than working on removing the 'clutter' for a clearer verbal explanation. Earlier in my career I did it because I was afraid of looking dumb; now it happens when I haven't taken enough time to prepare my presentation. Someone estimated that a good one-hour presentation takes about 30 hours to prepare. They are probably right.

Question time = fail

Being able to give a good performance during question time is a vital skill because it shows people what kind of academic you are when you are when you are off script. Unfortunately a lot of academics are old hands at asking tricky questions of research students – and they know all the brutal ones. The most common one in a confirmation presentations is "What is your research question?". It's an easy hit because usually the question (if there is one – rather than half a dozen) is so convoluted that it is easy to make fun of or rip to shreds. Sometimes it's merely the tone in which the question is delivered – of barely concealed derision – which is unnerving, especially to beginners. I think the key is to stay calm and take your time to answer. It can help to write the question on a piece of paper.

Endnote

While I was making this ebook I was surprised at the wealth of material I had generated in a year or so of blogging. There are many good posts which I left out in the interest of keeping this book brief and to the point. After this exercise in the curation and editing of my own writing I am even more convinced of the value of regular writing habits. Early posts required substantial editing and I was slightly embarrassed by the quality of my grammar in parts! Later posts required a lighter touch, which gives me hope that my writing style and technique has improved.

I can only encourage you to think about taking up the practice of blogging. Before I started the Thesis Whisperer I was certainly appreciated in my own home turf, but I was unknown outside. My role, in the central research office provided many opportunities to get out and about, teaching and talking with research students and their supervisors. I have been immersed in the business of managing research and research students in a large institution; all that experience has strongly informed what you read here. I am grateful that technological developments and the willingness of my managers to go along with this experiment in research education has enabled me to reach and talk to a global audience of research students like yourself. I hope this book has helped you on the journey and that we will talk sometime soon on www.thesiswhisperer.com

Recommended Reading

There's so many, many books on the market that claim to help you with your PhD – which ones are worth buying? I have been thinking about it this topic for some time, but it's still hard to decide. So here's a provisional top 5, based on books I use again and again in my PhD workshops and have referenced repeatedly in this book:

1. "The craft of Research" Wayne Booth, Greg Colomb and Joseph Williams.

I wish I owned the copyright to this one because I am sure they sell a shed load every year. Although it seems to be written for undergraduates, PhD students like it for its straight forward, unfussy style. Just about every aspect of research is covered: from considering your audience to planning and writing a paper (or thesis). The section on asking research questions is an excellent walk through of epistemology: an area many people find conceptually difficult. I find it speaks to both science and non science people, but, like all books I have encountered in the 'self help' PhD genre, *The Craft of Research* does have a bias towards 'traditional' forms of research practice. You creative researcher types might like to buy it anyway, if only to help you know what you are departing from.

2."How to Write a better thesis" by Paul Gruba and David Evans

This was the first book I ever bought on the subject, which probably accounts for my fondness for it. I have recommended it to countless students over the 6 or so years I have been Thesis Whispering, many of whom write to thank me. The appealing thing about this book is that it doesn't try to do too much. It sticks to the mechanics of writing a basic introduction> literature review> methods> results> conclusion style thesis, but I used it to write a project based creative research thesis when I did my masters and found the advice was still valid. Oh – and the price point is not bad either. If you can only afford one book on the list I would get this one.

3. "Helping Doctoral Students to write" by Barbara Kamler and Pat Thomson

I won an award for my thesis and this book is why. In *Helping doctoral students to write* Kamler and Thomson explain the concept of 'scholarly grammar', providing plenty of before and after examples which even the grammar disabled like myself can understand. I constantly recommend this book to students, but I find that one has to be at a certain stage in the PhD process to really hear what it has to say. I'm not sure why this is, but if you have been getting frustratingly vague feedback from your supervisors – who are unhappy but can't quite tell you why – you probably need to read this book. It is written for social science students, so scientists might be put off by the style – but please don't let that stop you from giving it a go. Physicists and engineers have told me they loved the book too. If you want a bit more of the conceptual basis behind the book, read this earlier post on why a thesis is a bit like an avatar.

4. "The unwritten rules of PhD research" by Marian Petre and Gordon Rugg

I love this book because it recognises the social complexities of doing a PhD, without ever becoming maudlin. Indeed it's genuinely funny in parts, which makes it a pleasure to read. The authors are at their best when explaining how academia works, such as the concept of 'sharks in the water' (the feeding frenzy sometimes witnessed in presentations when students make a mistake and are jumped on by senior academics) and the typology of supervisors. It's also one of the better references I have found on writing conference papers.

5. "Writing for social scientists" by Howard Becker

Reading this book is like sitting down in a comfy chair next to a kindly, old timey professor who is just going to tell you How It Is in academia in a pragmatic yet gentle fashion. Becker explains why the culture of academia - particularly power structures and social hierarchies - might be affecting your ability to write well and what to do about it. Despite the title, which suggests a limited audience, this book should be mandatory reading for every academic. The problems he describes are in no way restricted to the social scientists out there and the solutions will work for anyone.

Aside from these, the following books, papers and websites were referenced in the text and may be of interest for further study:

"5 emotions invented by the Internet" http://thoughtcatalog.com/2011/five-emotions-invented-by-the-internet/ accessed 28/01/2011

Browne, N. M & Keeley, S.M (2011) *Asking the Right Questions: A Guide to Critical Thinking* (10th Ed), Longman, New York.

Burt, R (2006) "The social origins of good ides, www.analytictech.com/mb709/readings/**burt**_SOGI.pdf *accessed 28/01/2012*

Clark, W (2006) *Academic charisma and the origins of the research university*, University of Chicago Press, Chicago.

Evans, T & Denholm, C (2006) *Doctorates Downunder: keys to successful doctoral study in Australia and New Zealand,* ACER Press, Camberwell.

Graff, G & Birkenstein, C (2009) They Say, I Say: The moves that matter in Academic Writing, W.W Norton and Company,

New York.

Kiley, M & Wisker, G (2009) *Threshold concepts in research education and evidence of threshold crossing*, Higher education research and development, v 28 (4) , pp 431 – 441

King, S (2010) *On Writing: 10th Anniversary Edition: a memoir of the craft*, Scribner, New York

Mullins, G. & Kiley, M (2002) *It's a PhD, not a Nobel Prize: how experienced examiners assess research theses*, Studies in Higher Education v27 (4), pp 369 - 384

Paltridge, B (2002) *Thesis and dissertation writing: an examination of published advice and actual practice*, English for specific purposes, v. 21 (2), pp 125 - 143

Phillips, E. M. & Pugh, D. S (2000) *How to get a PhD*, Open University Press, Maidenhead

Surowiecki, J (2011) A review of "The Thief of time", http://www.newyorker.com/arts/critics/books/2010/10/11/101011crbo_books_surowiecki Accessed 28/01/2012

Wurzman, R. S (2000) *Information Anxiety 2*, Que, New York.

---

[1] Evans, D., Gruba, P. & Zobel, J (2012) How

to write a better thesis (3rd Ed), Melbourne
University Press, Melbourne